MW00647915

step-by-step guide. It is the book I wish I had when I became a new dad." Robin Grille, father, Psychologist, author, <u>Parenting for a Peaceful World</u> & <u>Heart to Heart Parenting</u>

"It is so easy to digest. I'm already brainstorming about my birth preparation classes and how to make more 'room' for the fathers. This is the book I have been looking for." Eydis Hentze, mother, doula (birth coach)

"A genuine, insightful book that reveals the basic truths and addresses the complex issues men experience as expectant fathers. It is also a great resource for moms and health professionals." Hogan Hilling, 'stay-at-home' dad, educator & co-author, <u>The Modern Mom's Guide to Dads</u>

"It has an optimistic and joyous tone, very useful for many dads and families." Yehudi Gordon MD, Obstetrician, father & author, <u>Birth and Beyond</u> & <u>The Encyclopedia of Pregnancy and Birth</u>

"It opens not only your mind, but your heart. It should be read aloud to every pregnant mother by her partner while they forge ahead together into the world of childrearing." Barbara Harper, RN, CLD, CCE, mother, Founder/Director Waterbirth International

"A brilliant handbook for any father-to-be – full of wisdom and insight'", Adrienne Burgess, mother, author, <u>Fatherhood Reclaimed</u>

"Patrick Houser's <u>Fathers-To-Be Handbook</u> is a breath of fresh air and long overdue. This powerful little volume is must reading for all fathers." Christiane Northrup, MD, mother, author <u>Mother-Daughter Wisdom</u>.

"The handbook outlines in a very clear and linear fashion what it entails to become a father. You are led beyond all the pitfalls and fears that many men encounter, and you are given essential tools for the journey." Douglas Crawford, Life Coach & Trainer

"A refreshing departure from the all-to-often patronizing and jokey books for expectant dads. Houser encourages a more reflective, intuitive approach to fatherhood. A must read for anyone interested in more than assembling nursery furniture and changing diapers" Leah Hazard, mother, doula, author, <u>The Fathers Home Birth Handbook</u>

"A must read for all fathers-to-be. A superb guide for understanding the father-mother-child relationship; truly informative, inspirational and enlightening." Richard Branson, future father, publisher, <u>Wellbeing Magazine</u>

"It's an important and missing piece, and will help many men make the transition to fatherhood." William Emerson PhD, father, teacher, writer.

"Throughout the text, which combines interesting research with anecdotes, it retains a delightful, personal feel, as if you're in conversation with the author. He dares to push a few boundaries to help a man extend his view into parenting, and indeed life." Veronika Robinson, mother, editor <u>The Mother Magazine</u>, author, <u>The Drinks Are On Me</u>

FATHERS-TO-BE HANDBOOK

A Road Map for the
Transition to Fatherhood

Patrick M. Houser

Creative Life Systems

First published in United States on January 5, 2009 by
Creative Life Systems, 193 Mariner
South Portland, Maine 04106
www.ceativelifesystems.com

First published in Great Britain in 2007 by Creative Life Systems
6 Court Lodge, Lamberhurst, Kent TN3 8DU

Library of Congress Control Number: 2008910331

ISBN: 978-0-615-23338-3

1.Fathers-Psychology. 2.Husbands-Psychology. 3.Mothers-Psychology.
4.Wives-Psychology. 5.Parenting.

Houser, Patrick M., 1948
Fathers to be handbook, a roadmap for the transition to fatherhood/
Patrick M. Houser

1st ed.
Printed on recycled paper by BookMasters
Ashland, Ohio

Front cover photo: Getty Images-Stephen Marks
Back cover photo: Steen Larsen, www.steenlarsen.dk

Dedicated To All Families

Contents

Preface

I came of age in the 1960's in the United States. Although my family was traditional, I was blessed with a high level of curiosity at a time of great social change. I asked why and why not, how and how come, and who says so? I took the road less travelled. After graduating from university, I explored for several years throughout the US and Mexico. In a way, I have always continued the spirit of my journey that began back then. I have lived in various regions and countries. I have lived in England since 1998.

Until I was ten I grew up on a 200 acre farm in Ohio. I was the third of what would become a family of six children. We lived on a hill in a large, brick farmhouse with a white fence around it. There was a stream below for fishing and getting wet. We were surrounded by woods and pastures, wild life and farm animals. There were fields and barns to explore and play in. The setting was idyllic and liberating.

When my time came to become a father it was the mid-seventies. I was twenty-eight and living in the very rural Missouri Ozarks; we went 'back to the land'. My then wife, Kathryn, and I planned a homebirth. We enrolled the services of an experienced and big hearted midwife, the wonderfully named Mau Blossom. I was an eager and willing participant in every aspect of the pregnancy and birth; that a man could be. We prepared ourselves, as best we knew how, and anticipated the arrival of our child. Until my participation at the birth of my first child none of the men in my family had attended one.

Kathryn's labor was a long and hard 36 hours with 12 hours of pushing. The birth of our son, Anandas, did not follow the plan we had imagined. The delivery was intense and there were complications. It was distressing.

The emotional impact that the birth had on us was significant. We wondered if there was more to the process of birth than we were aware of which could have had an effect on the result. We had already learned that what we thought about life could have an effect on our daily experience of it. However, we had not yet made the connection as to how birth could be similarly affected. We also sensed that our physical and emotional experience was not an isolated one. We knew there was more to learn. In the years that followed I made an extensive and wide-ranging enquiry. Through self-exploration and the study of birth and birth psychology I learned much about myself, birth and our culture.

I found that very little real attention was being paid to this most fundamental, yet influential, of human events. Birth has been treated as something to get through or over and acknowledged primarily on a physical level, for babies and parents. The actual human experience we are each having has been largely ignored.

In October 1980, this time after a ninety minute labor, Kathryn gave birth to our second son Jeremy, in water and into my hands, at home. This was the first documented water-birth in the United States.

Second births are often easier and have shorter labors. However, we were moved by the contrast of our personal experience of this birth compared to the first one. In the lead-up to Jeremy's birth we focused considerable attention on our inner preparation. We felt this supported our experience and the outcome considerably.

We had also opened the doorway to a gentler and more physically supportive method of birthing by incorporating water into the delivery. What had begun as an urge to create a more supportive and welcoming environment for our baby (and his mother), later became part of a pioneering initiative to bring attention to and improve birthing practices internationally.

I have supported numerous births over the years and counseled parents and others to explore their own experiences and beliefs. Although I have had other interests and careers, a reoccurring theme in my life has been to support greater awareness about birthing our children and our families.

Towards this end, I have co-founded a UK Registered Charity (The SOURCE Foundation International) to expand education and understanding into this field. And now, together with my colleague Elmer Postle, I work specifically with fathers, mothers, childbirth professionals/educators, doulas and family oriented organizations through our initiative, Fathers-To-Be. Our work is based on many of the principles in this book. I also lecture and present workshops in various formats throughout the world.

We have also begun a world-wide campaign, *One Baby – Two Parents, supporting early parenthood.* This educational campaign is designed to help raise everyone's awareness of and support for the whole family during the all important foundational time. Fathers, as yet, are an underutilized and unsupported resource who have 24/7 influence over a mother and child. Our fathers deserve support for the crucially important role they provide.

I came to fathering with wide-eyed innocence. I have been disappointed and felt helpless on occasion. I have tried to run away at times. I also feel blessed beyond words for the gifts my children have bestowed on me by their presence and their love. I have found that my early commitment and involvement cemented our bond in a way that has consistently shown the way through to loving.

I have learned that the experiences babies are having during pregnancy, birth and the first year are significant contributors to who they will become emotionally, intellectually, physically and spiritually. I have also developed a deep understanding and appreciation for the experience mothers and fathers are having during this transition time.

Fathers today are taking part in the family in more ways than ever before. Consequently, society has a unique opportunity. Fathers can speak for this and future generations through their loving participation with their children and in their family. This book gives a voice to my experiences, discoveries and visions for the future.

Introduction

Fathers Make A World Of Difference

"Of all nature's gifts to the human race,
what is sweeter to a man than his children?"

Cicero

A new father has arrived.

For millennia birth has been almost exclusively the domain of women; men had a different more distant role to play. For the first time in our history most fathers are participating in the birth of their children. They are also expanding their involvement in the modern family. Fathers today face new challenges because of this. The information, ideas and tools provided in this handbook can assist expectant and new dads in their transition to fatherhood.

You will discover
- Techniques for reducing stress during pregnancy and birth.
- Modern ways to protect and provide for your family.
- Information on how to participate more effectively during the pregnancy.
- Ideas regarding contributing to your child's wellbeing, even now.
- Guidance for bringing a calm and useful presence to your partner's labor and to the birth of your child.
- How to take part in building strong and loving foundations for your child which will augment their entire lifetime.

The result is that you will be better prepared to participate in the most joyful, satisfying and empowering time of your life.

Help with all those questions

Once a woman reveals her pregnancy to her partner, and reality dawns for the man, virtually all fathers-to-be will ponder the same thing:

"She is having a baby.
What am I supposed to be doing?"

This book will help you to resolve this and various other questions like:

- What about sex during pregnancy and the breastfeeding time?
- What is it like to adopt a more nurturing relationship with a child?
- When I think about becoming a father I notice I get anxious. What do I do?
- My father was not so great. How can I be a different kind of father?
- How am I going to be remembered as a father? Do I have a choice?

Opportunity

We will consider conception onward to early infancy through the minds and hearts of the developing baby, the mother and the father. This will provide an understanding of how each family member can be supported, care for each other and receive the most benefit from every phase of this precious time together.

You can awaken your natural fathering instincts as well as acquire the knowledge that will support your development as a father. A central theme in this book is to explore modern possibilities for a father's role in today's family. You do not need to be limited by the stereotypes of what a father used to be or should be. You can decide for yourself.

A father's role is important

The nature of a father's involvement, from the start, has significant impact on a child's development in numerous ways. "Where fathers are involved, breastfeeding is more successful, post-natal depression reduced, children are more successful at examinations at 16 and are less likely to have a criminal record at 21."[1]

There are volumes of research which confirm:

Fathers make a world of difference.

A once in a lifetime opportunity exists, now. Through research in science and psychology, we now know that the baby is having significant and lasting experiences during pregnancy, birth and the early months of life. They are also aware and making decisions about these experiences. The weight of those decisions can influence a lifetime.

A woman, during this significant and very special time is birthing a child, a family and our society. She needs to be protected and provided for in ways that recognize the importance of her role.

Men are also having an experience during this time which deserves to be acknowledged and supported. Men's experience is different than women's. Men feel, yet they sense and interpret feelings differently from women. Men also reveal and resolve their feelings in dissimilar ways. Fathers have a particular role to play and they can benefit greatly from specific guidance and support, just like mothers.

This book is to inform but also to stimulate an enquiry. Who are we, how did we come to be this way and what do we, as fathers, really want for ourselves and our families?

The research, tools and exercises herein are designed to help you in resolving concerns or ambivalence you may have surrounding pregnancy, birth and fathering. This will result in less stress for all and increased confidence and enjoyment for you and your partner.

What is provided here can be used as a road map. Like any map, this one will indicate numerous possible routes to use to help you get to where you would like to be, as a father to your children and contributor in your family.

Mothers can also derive great benefit from this book. A simple word change from father to mother and man to woman will reveal much.

1

A Road Map For Fathers

"My father didn't tell me how to live;
he lived, and let me watch him do it."

Clarence B. Kelland

She has made the announcement. You are to be a father. Actually, you already are a father; the baby is simply not visible yet. Your child, a living, loving being, is in your partner's womb.

Fathering may well be unknown and unexplored territory for you. To have help navigating can be very useful. Having the use of certain tools and perhaps even a compass could also be invaluable.

You may have varied and conflicting thoughts about becoming a father. The largest percentage of pregnancies are not explicitly planned. The nature of this fact carries with it the inevitability of surprise and possibly uncertainty.

Expectant dads respond to pregnancy in a wide variety of ways. You may still have some lingering questions.

- Is this the person I want to spend the rest of my life with?
- Is this the right point in my life to be having a child?
- We already have children, do we really want more?
- What about career timing, for my partner and me?
- Are we financially prepared?

- What if we are not married?
- Is our house big enough?
- What about my freedom?

These and other issues may be of concern to you. You will be given opportunities throughout this book to resolve them. What is important, firstly, is how you feel and think about your concerns. Speaking with your partner can help each of you to become more comfortable.

Acceptance of the pregnancy will provide you with the opportunity to experience more joy at the prospect of being a father. This is a precious moment for you. Life will never be the same as it was; and that is really good news.

One thing that can support your acceptance of the pregnancy is to consider the possibility that your baby loves you already. What would you do differently if you were certain that your baby loved you, right now? What if you proceed with this assumption? Can you embrace your relationship with your child, now? Remind yourself regularly, "My baby loves me", and notice how it feels and affects your thoughts and actions.

Power Tools for Fathering

This can be the most profound and empowering time of your life. There may well be elements that border on the mystical. It can also be a most challenging period. The time of pregnancy and birth can be seen as a growing time. While a baby's growth is most obvious, parents are often going to experience growth of a different nature. You are in one of life's most significant transitions and change will be constant. This will require flexibility on your part. Your personal growth during pregnancy and birth can seem like a forced march if you resist the process or are not sufficiently supported.

Throughout this book you will find various tools, exercises and information to support you. Feel free to explore the content and delve however deeply you wish to go with the different elements. This book is designed in such a way that you could spend anywhere from ninety minutes to nine months with it. Feel free to take your time and perhaps take breaks to integrate what you are learning. If you notice you are becoming uneasy, pause and take a deep breath.

There are times in the text when an exercise is presented; a horizontal line will distinguish them. Please feel free to do these as and when you choose. You may wish to work with the exercises as you go along. You could also read straight through the book and come back to them later. Some topics you may wish to revisit and work with more than once or over a period of time. Many of the Power Tools for fathering are briefly introduced next.

Affirmations are positive statements asserting that a goal a person wishes to achieve has already happened. They can be very useful during preparation for being a father. Affirmations can support you in changing your thinking and long held beliefs about life and fathering. An affirmation can be spoken, written or mentally projected.

Breathing and Meditation are ancient practices that can also be valuable modern resources during your transition to fatherhood. A very simple form of meditation will be presented to support you to calm your mind and relax your body. You can also learn to regulate your breathing to reduce stress.

Choice is one of life's most powerful features. Fathering will bring with it many and varied choices. What do you expect your fathering to be like? Do you have any control over this or is the outcome inevitable? Can you choose to do it differently from your father? What would that look like? The interesting thing about choice is that until you know you have options, and what they are, you do not actually have a conscious choice. Are you choosing what you really want? The ultimate choice is to choose what you are thinking. How are you investing your mental resources and is this investment paying you back with dividends you actually want?

Empathy and Listening are valuable qualities to develop during this time. They will also serve you well for years to come. Do your best to imagine what this experience is like for your partner, particularly if this is her first pregnancy. Be willing to expand your capacity for being patient and loving. Listening can be extremely important. Listening is done with the ears and the heart, never with the mouth. Be willing to support her silently, at times.

Father's Circle is an exercise I have designed specially for fathers based on Neuro-Linguistic Programming (NLP). NLP is a body of information about how the human mind works and how people think. Utilizing it you can bring about desired changes faster and more easily.

Father's Compass is a metaphorical as well as a practical tool. You will be guided in the use of one to support you in navigating fatherhood.

Forgiveness is a gift for you. By forgiving someone else you make a choice to free yourself from resentment and blame. Forgiving someone does not absolve them of responsibility for their actions. You just decide to move on. Letting go of old issues is good for everyone, particularly you. Forgiving can help you to become a better father.

Gratitude is invaluable. Being grateful for everything, past or present, is powerful and will expand your experience of love. Gratitude for your father can be tremendously healing. For some, this may require a little work to achieve; but you can do it. Gratitude will open you to receiving more of whatever it is you want for yourself.

You may find it beneficial to start a Father's Journal. This is a dedicated notebook, a private place for you to record your thoughts and inner explorations regarding your fathering, on an ongoing basis. You could begin writing now. What do you think about what you have read so far? How do you feel?

2

Fathering Throughout Time

"We make a living by what we get,
but we make a life by what we give."

Winston Churchill

Protect and Provide For

The fundamental nature of a father's role had changed little over time, until recently. Fathers have traditionally had the role of protecting and providing for their families. Protecting used to include guarding against danger: wild animals or intruders. The form and setting of providing has varied greatly from forest, to field, to factory, to office. Fathers worked and they brought back the results of their work; food, goods and money. These archetypal roles were in the context of a clan, tribe or village. Fathers, primarily, had been giving various forms of physical support. Perhaps today's fathers can offer a different type of protection; and providing for has new forms as well.

A modern interpretation of 'to protect and provide for' could include the environment of the pregnancy and birth. Reading, attending classes and participating with your partner will provide her with valuable support. She will likely need and appreciate it in the early months. Connecting with your child, while he is in the womb, and actively bonding also sends signals to your partner that you are devoted to your new family. This is very important for a mother-to-be. Also included in your role could be making sure the birth environment itself is comfortable, calm and safe. With the trend towards 'medicalized' and industrialized birthing practices you may also want to protect your family in more unexpected ways.

Women's Movement

The women's movement peaked during the second half of the 20th century and much change ensued. Women wanted recognition for their contribution to the family and society, more freedom, and different role and life options. The rigidity of our archetypal patriarchy was limiting the freedom of both women and men. The women's movement can perhaps be credited with evolving our culture by stimulating changes to the historic straight jacket of gender roles.

Now, men have been liberated as well. Not all men have embraced these cultural shifts. If we have not had family role models or support for such changes these transitions could be confusing and disconcerting. Men and women now have greater equality in relationships, careers and community life. As a result, the character of the family has changed forever.

Nuclear Family

The cultural evolution to the nuclear family has left a hole where a family's support systems used to be. There is a proverb which says, "It takes a village to raise a child". Our villages, towns and cities no longer provide the spirit, much less the meaning, behind this saying. Families do not have the wide-ranging support that was previously customary in tribes and villages. Mothers have historically had their mother, grandmother, in-laws or midwife for role models and support for having a baby and raising a family. This gap has been partially filled by an extensive network of resources to support and educate mothers-to-be. This is invaluable for mothers; however fathers have yet to be afforded the same opportunity.

These shifting cultural trends of the last fifty years, however, have brought men more fully into the family and included them at a more personal level than ever before. This is invaluable as a starting place for understanding fatherhood today.

Changing Family Roles

Today's society has changed significantly. One change is the blurred line that differentiates gender roles. In the majority of families today both parents have jobs. This alone can cause a shift in parents' roles. Most couples have their own unique design for how they cooperate economically, socially and within the family. These contemporary shifts have modified the structure of the family and virtually assures role changes, and sometimes role reversals. "In one third of the families today where pre-school children are at home and a parent is the caregiver, it is the father."[2]

My own family history was representative of the time. The fathers worked in the fields or businesses and the mothers were housewives, exclusively. The women took responsibility for virtually all aspects of home and family life, especially raising the children. Mothers not only raised the children, they and the children were to a large degree the family unit. The fathers did their time at work and in society, and they came and went from the family.

Though fathers were a part of the family, they did not participate in raising the children in every day life. The mothers interrelated with every aspect of the children's lives from health care and education, to meals, clothing and their social lives. The fathers then learned about the children from the mothers. Although fathers were considered to be 'raising the family', they were on the outside looking in, to a large degree.

The one exception to the mothers' governance in the family was regarding discipline. Many children of this era were told, "Just wait until your father gets home" or something similar. We all knew what that meant. This was like a stay of execution and, as you can imagine, the rest of the day would not go so well. The father would come home, perhaps tired and frustrated from a days work, and the mother would recall to him the particulars of who needed discipline for what wrong doing. The father would then portion it out. This was one method of keeping children in line. It also placed an unreasonable burden on the father and child relationship.

If a father is working and earning money, there can still be a strong, traditional providing component to his contribution. Women, however, have also stepped up to help fill this previously male function. A father's family role today has also expanded to include more activities that were formerly of the mother's domain. This includes everything from direct caretaking and nurturing to diaper changing.

When you provide material and nurturing support your presence and commitment will have profound and lasting value. This whole hearted, lifetime commitment will brighten your darkest days and glorify the brilliant ones.

Fathering in a Modern Age

Perhaps the most significant feature of modern fathering is dad's participation during the pregnancy of his partner, birth of their children and early parenting. Mothers today usually want fathers to be more involved and in most instances they are.

Men's archetypal model, as well as their own upbringing, has primarily conditioned them to do the basic physical activities. Fathers are rapidly, and often haphazardly, trying to figure out how to successfully engage in new ways. They are eager for a different type of involvement and can do more for their families, especially when they are properly supported.

On our first prenatal visit with our midwife, Mau introduced me to the concept that I was also 'pregnant'. This was a 'brain stopper' for me and it clicked. From that moment on I adopted the stance that I was also having this baby. I believe it allowed me to more easily engage with Kathryn's pregnancy and our child and to begin fathering. It benefited my whole family. Kathryn was carrying our baby and I was carrying our family. I understood that by caring for her I was also caring for our child. I was no longer a bystander, baggage handler or just the sperm donor. I was embracing my new fathering role at an early stage.

Men are most receptive to learning at this time of becoming a father. This opening has an opportunity implicit in it. "Research consensus recognizes that the more extensive a father's emotional investment, attachment, involvement and provision of resources, the more his child benefits in cognitive competence, school performance, empathy, self-esteem, self-control, well-being, life skills and social competence. So there is much to be gained by a father's capable, committed and loving involvement."[3]

I have found that many men today have not attended any classes beyond their formal education or training for a career. They are however eager to learn about becoming a father, in a way that works for them. Fathers today are willing to cross the bridge from a life of only providing physical support to one of being more emotionally involved in their family.

Currently, fathers are rarely provided with their own preparation opportunity. There are some couples classes or a dad's segment within a mother's class being offered. However, these forums are designed by women and taught by women. They provide information primarily to educate and support mothers. Most men tell me that, although informative, they did not feel welcome and it was not particularly satisfying for them. This is simply how birth education has developed. There is rarely a space for just fathers to come together to receive information and support designed specifically for fathers and taught by fathers. Fathers-To-Be is changing that.

As I work with fathers in our Fathers-To-Be

groups I find that they enjoy exploring and learning about this new phase of their lives. These events are distinctly different from typical men's groups. Fathers come together to learn about a specialized aspect of manhood; becoming a father. They share a desire to learn about new possibilities for themselves and their families. Men often have concerns, questions and gaps in their understanding of how to be as a father in today's family and society.

For men, being in a room with other fathers enhances their willingness and ability to trust and be honest about what they are thinking and feeling. Men have an emotional literacy, contrary to the stereotype. Fathers are relieved to hear from other fathers. Sharing stories, acknowledging they are having a deep personal experience and just being heard can sometimes make all the difference. It is about freeing the father, in the man.

Through our Fathers-To-Be website we are supporting dads coming together in living rooms around the world. The importance and significance of fathers' groups can not be overstated. To be able to hear from and speak with others in a similar situation is profound. These 'Father2Father' groups will be mostly informal and hosted by *volunteer* fathers who appreciate the value of peer support. Fathers supporting fathers, mentoring each other, has the possibility to transform our culture.

3

Freeing The Father

Preparation

"My father gave me the greatest gift anyone could give another person, he believed in me."

Jim Valvano

Gifts from Our Fathers

We have each received gifts from our father. There were the material gifts, perhaps toys or sporting gear. Also there were the non-physical gifts. Did your dad spend time with you? Did he take the time to personally support you in things that were important to you? Did he believe in you? What messages did he give you about who you are? Here we will reflect on the non-physical gifts, rather than the material ones.

A variety of these gifts have been received knowingly and some unknowingly. The gifts we received from our father may have seemed like a shiny, red bicycle or perhaps they felt more like a rusty old bike with a flat tire and a bent wheel, metaphorically speaking. Maybe they were wonderful, endearing and cherished or possibly not. 'Negative gifts' you received could be having an ongoing detrimental effect. If left unresolved, events from our past can affect our life and relationships indefinitely.

The opportunity here is to integrate the gifts, regardless of their nature. If you are to discover their value it may necessitate an unwrapping and close examination of them in order to decide how they can be useful to you now, as an adult. The gifts from your father may have included love, support and encouragement or criticism, anger and blame. More likely than not, you received a combination. What if you were able to embrace the gifts, and the giver, and thereby receive value from them? For those who received what seemed like unloving gifts this may not always be an easy process, and it is possible.

The following exercise can help. Judge for yourself how deeply you want to go into the questions raised and explorations into your background. If there are deep, unresolved issues you may want to consult with a counselor. This is just the beginning of our exploration. Throughout this book your enquiry will be guided by the use of various techniques. Whatever type of fathering you received, you have the ability to work through issues and resolve them so you can feel more confident about your own fathering.

You may wish to write a list of the gifts you received from your father. Perhaps divide it into two lists; one of the cherished and empowering gifts and another of the ones that seem unsettled for you. This may include specific memories or general feelings and thoughts.

Fathering School

We each had an upbringing which was one of a kind. No one else had the same one, not even our siblings. We were each conceived, spent time in the womb and were born and raised under unique circumstances. We also arrived at different times in our fathers' life as an individual and as a father. As such, we have each had different influences.

This time growing up could be compared to going to school. Your father was the lead teacher in your fathering school. You were taught about fathering by your father. It was virtually the same as if you had been learning accounting, in accounting school, except it was typically for a much more extended period of time and imprinted at a deeper emotional level. Imagine attending the same school for eighteen years and every day you have a lesson on one particular subject; fathering. Some days the lesson was explicit; other times it was more subtle. Fathering may have been your favorite class. You may have had an outstanding teacher who treated you with love and respect. Perhaps you were even his favorite student. Or it could have been an unpleasant experience for you and not your favorite class, or teacher for that matter. For most, it was probably a mixture. In any case your father was giving lessons and you were receiving them.

A review of your fathering curriculum could prove valuable. View the teaching you received as your career training for fatherhood. You may want to do some review or post graduate studies in order to have more freedom in your choices about being the kind of father you want to be.

You could take this opportunity to contemplate or write about what you think you learned from your father. What was your childhood like? What was your father like, and your relationship with him? How was your father's relationship with your mother? How did he treat her? What was your father's relationship to your family? Spending time reflecting on these questions could be quite enlightening for you. Often, answers are available to us when we ask the right questions. You may wish to speak with your father about this, if possible. You could also write and explore some of these questions in an autobiographical way. Feel free to do this as and when it suits you.

According to Dr. Thomas Verny, a psychiatrist and pioneer in the field of prenatal and birth psychology: "Findings in the peer-reviewed literature over the course of decades establish, beyond any doubt, that parents have overwhelming influence on the mental and physical attributes of the children they raise." This influence *begins before* the children are born, not after. In his groundbreaking book, <u>The Secret Life of the Unborn Child</u> he states further: "New research is also beginning to focus much more on the father's feelings. Until recently his emotions were disregarded. Our latest studies indicate that this view is dangerously wrong. They show that how a man feels about his wife and unborn child is one of the single most important factors in determining the success of a pregnancy."[4]

Walk a Mile in Dad's Shoes

Another useful insight to consider is where your father was coming from, literally. He may not have had the best relationship with his father. This may have affected the way he was with you and your family.

There were eight of us in my family. We were as much a team as a family. I learned about relationships and co-operation from an early age. My father, Jim, was the friendliest man I have ever known. In our home town, as he drove down the street, he would wave to virtually everyone who went past. He did not necessarily know each person, it was just his nature. His friendliness, however, was not always experienced by his own family.

In the early years my father was very involved in our family. He engaged in play and evening activities; baths and bedtime. However, as our numbers increased and we got older, we moved from the farm where I had grown up and my father went to work for his father. My grandfather had an automobile dealership and my father was the service manager. Although my grandfather was loving with his grandchildren, he was persistently critical towards my father. He belittled him constantly. Anger was my grandfather's most common method of communicating with him. This deeply affected my dad. His resulting conduct in our family often wavered between expressing his anger, toward his children, and disappearing (physically and/or emotionally) so he would 'do no harm'.

Their relationship had a knock-on effect, often experienced literally by my siblings and me. When my father dispensed discipline (aka corporal punishment), it was often fuelled with his frustration and resulting anger. This left us with an experience of what I call a 'Father's Cloud' over my family. The way in which my father related to his children was affected by how his father related to him. I also perceive that my father felt insecure about his participation in our family because of the harmful effects he caused at times. It was this insecurity which resulted in his 'disappearing'.

As I reflect on my own fathering I recognize that there were times when I would find ways to disappear from my children. I would watch television or find excuses to not participate with them. Although this was mild in comparison, and there was no aggression, I can sense the family origins. For much of my children's early childhood I was a stay at home dad and was very involved in their daily lives. However, I often felt insecure about how to be with them.

The saving grace for my siblings and me was that my father and mother were deeply in love. One expression of that love was their love for their children, which they gave us generously. My father was a great and loving contributor to my life for whom I am deeply grateful. He wanted to be a 'good' father and I think he did the best he could with what he had *inherited* from his own father.

Know that your father was probably working with what his father had given him. What characteristics do you think you have inherited from your father that have become part of your personal landscape? Let's redefine family inheritance to include matters of the heart and bequeath to our children gifts of love and joy, strength and tenderness. Be certain about what you want to pass on to your children and make clear choices about that.

The Power of Choice

Some men face varying degrees of apprehension about fathering. This can be because of their personal experiences or perhaps a lack of information. I have known two men who had vasectomies at a young age because of their personal fears about the possibility of 'becoming their father'. They were not going to risk doing to another what had been done to them. The nature of their particular action was radical to say the least. They did not know how to 'unlearn' what their fathers taught them and they did not trust themselves. They thought they had no choice. Rest assured, you do.

This raises the question, will I become like my father? If you had a great dad who did everything you could hope for to support you and provide you with ideal fathering you would, more likely than not, follow a similar direction with your own children. You would carry out the fathering training you had received. If you are trained as an accountant, you do accounting and you do it the way you were taught, with variations of course. This ideal father scenario is not always the case. Many of us had an upbringing by our fathers that was lacking in a variety of ways. This could have included ambivalence, neglect, disapproval, physical and/or emotional abuse, disrespect and abandonment.

Even if your father disappeared early on, or was absent in other ways like mine, that action and others had an effect on you. You made decisions about fathering as a result of how you were fathered. You may not be aware of these decisions because often they are held in the subconscious mind. When you are becoming a father, these unconscious patterns can surface. If they do, typically one of two things will happen. One possibility is that you pass them on to your children, through unconscious behavior. Another is that you bring them into your conscious awareness and work on resolving them so this does not happen. Shortly, you will be provided with various tools to help you move past such challenges. You can then make decisions, in awareness, and have more choices about how you are with your children.

In a counseling session I received years ago I uncovered an unresolved issue from when I was a teenager. There was this great black and chrome motorcycle that I wanted. Since quite young I delivered newspapers and did odd jobs for money. I was good at saving money so I could afford the motorcycle and I really, really wanted it. My parents had forbidden me to purchase the motorcycle. I argued but to no avail. I was angry and felt controlled by them.

During the course of my session I released my long held upset. For all of the years in between I had no conscious recall of my hurt. In the session I also became aware that my parents were acting out of love, for my safety. They were concerned I would be injured, or worse. My original interpretation had been quite different. I had felt helpless and powerless at the time and thought that *it was not fair*. What followed the session was my calling them, in an emotional state, and expressing my gratitude for all they had done for me throughout my life. They were a bit confused by the call yet grateful; the gift of their love was being received. I did not mention the motorcycle as that was my issue, not theirs. What was important was that I had removed an unconscious barrier I had to loving them more fully. There could now be more love experienced between us.

This event may not seem paramount; however it was unresolved for me. Many of us have issues to contend with regarding our upbringing. We can learn to resolve them, dissipate our attachment to them, and thus their residual effect on us. Tremendous freedom is available to us when we let go of old emotional baggage. We all have the ability to heal past injuries and move on.

We can learn how to turn what looks like a liability into an asset, a true gift. Using affirmations, attending classes and reading, speaking with your parents and counseling can all help you to resolve past negative influences. We have the option to truly receive the gifts from our fathers, in love. He may not have known that he had a choice or the support to make one, as you do. You have the possibility to do your fathering exactly how you want to.

Affirmations

There is a saying that a man's children and his garden both reflect the amount of weeding done during the growing season. Affirmations can work similarly to weeding your garden. They help you to thin out undesirable thoughts, which took root at an earlier time. As you use an affirmation negative thoughts or feelings can be brought to the surface, like weeds to be removed. The affirmation then takes root, as a new positive thought. Affirmations help you to reframe your experiences, and any decisions you made about them, and start fresh.

Affirmations should always state what you want, as opposed to what you do not want. For example, *"I am a good father"*, rather than, *"I do not want to be a bad father"*. Research shows our mind does not integrate 'not', and tends to not 'hear' it. Reread the second statement above, leaving out the not, and you will understand the importance of this detail. I encourage you to embrace affirmations and the support they can give you in fathering.

Work with one affirmation at a time. Choose one, write it, pause... take a breath... 'listen in for a response' and write out the response. Allow yourself to be open to any response; thoughts, feelings or sensations in your body. If you do not detect a response after a pause, simply write the affirmation again and continue. Resist any temptation to 'censor' your responses to the affirmation. Then pause, take a breath and write the affirmation again, and your response, and again. Repeat the exploration over and over. There is no prescribed number. Notice how you feel and what you are thinking. Your response could be the same each time; however it will typically evolve and change. Be patient. Here are some sample affirmations for you to use for the transition to fatherhood.

- I always know how to best support my partner and my child.
- I always know how to best support myself.
- This is the perfect time for a new baby to come into my life.
- I am the perfect father for my child.
- I am a capable and gifted father.
- My partner is safe.
- My baby is safe.
- I trust myself.
- Birth is safe
- I am safe.

You could work with one affirmation for minutes, hours or days. This is a process which develops. As your responses change you may be inspired to modify or alter the affirmation or shift to a wholly new affirmation. Engage with an open mind so as to inspire a new way of thinking about yourself and your fathering. You could also work together with your partner on this and encourage her to use affirmations to support her mothering.

I also recommend you assign affirmations to your mind. Choose a phrase to hold mentally and to repeat regularly throughout the day. This is also very effective at improving your daily outlook in general.

There are numerous opportunities throughout this book which will reveal affirmations for you to utilize. I encourage you to explore the benefit of using affirmations regularly. Often the more you use a particular *tool*, the better you get at working with it. Over the years, I have known people who completely transformed their lives through the use of affirmations alone. Affirmations are true Power Tools.

Forgiveness

Many years ago I worked with a client named John. He told me that he had hated his father all of his life. John was committed to never having children as a result of the abuse he had received from his father. John's relationship with his father was a burning issue for him, which was why he came to me. I mentioned the value of forgiveness, for him personally as well as his relationship with his father. He was not the least bit interested.

John's session was powerful and deep. His father featured strongly. During the session he released a significant amount of anger and, ultimately, felt some sadness regarding his relationship with his father. Near the end of his session I asked him if he could forgive his father for the way he had treated him. His response was, *"Never"*. I then asked if he would be willing to consider forgiving his father at some point in the future. He said, *"Not a chance"*. So, I then inquired if he would consider that at some time in the future he might be willing to think about the possibility of forgiving his father. *"I'll think about it",* was his answer, with a very slight grin. This was a successful first step, for John. We all need to start where we are.

If you had a great father, who you felt participated brilliantly in your life, then fathering may come naturally to you. There may also have been unloving aspects of your relationship with your dad. This could cause you to create a *Father's Cloud* around your participation with your children. It could also prevent you from feeling welcome and capable in your role as a father. Forgiveness can work wonders toward healing unresolved issues.

Forgiveness clears the slate. It takes you out of the blame and resentment games that are common if you are holding something against another. It frees up your mind, your energy and your capacity to love and be loved.

Healing begins the moment we make a new choice. Forgiving is one such choice. An important element of forgiveness can include forgiving yourself. You may be holding something against yourself; resolving it is important and forgiveness can help. Do you have any unresolved issues with your partner, or a partner from the past? Now is a good time to clean up any relationship history you may have. Unresolved past events can be burdensome and cause stress which you may or may not be aware of. Forgiveness is an important element of resolution.

You may wish to explore through contemplation or by writing the affirmations, "I forgive my father" and "I forgive my father for...". Also, "I forgive my mother" or anyone else who emerges as having had a significant influence in your life. Explore with awareness and sensitivity. Try, "I forgive myself". Write the phrase then pause and listen for a response and then write whatever you hear, think or feel. This will allow a clearing effect in your mind and emotions. Repeat as necessary and vary the phrases as you are moved to, i.e. "I forgive myself for..." or "I forgive myself for something I did or did not do".

If we are willing to work our way through

anger, judgments and resentments we can find the love. Often, people who act less than kind in their words and actions do so because they feel insecure, afraid or inadequate. They are often making a cry for help and want to heal but do not know how to. Many people who have been hurt tend to go on and hurt others, until they decide to break the cycle and choose to love themselves and others. "Forgiveness is the key to happiness", as <u>A Course in Miracles</u> says.[5]

Gratitude

Expanding gratitude can also be powerful at this time. Gratitude for your partner is most obvious. And of course gratitude for this magnificent child who has come to grace your life and love you completely.

A friend of mine, Terry, received a phone call from her sister who had been on holiday. Terry's sister told her that she had purchased a gift for her and would give it to her when they next met. Terry immediately expressed heart-felt gratitude to her sister. Terry had not yet received the gift nor did she even know what it was. She was, however, already receiving an aspect of the gift, which was the love it represented.

Gratitude is a gift we offer to the giver and one that we receive as well. Gratitude usually causes everyone to feel good too. Expressing gratitude, whether you are actually experiencing it yet or not, can clear the way to feeling grateful. Gratitude for the non-physical gifts in our life is most powerful. This may include: people, love, health, trust, beauty, nature, art, music and more. Recall for a moment a time in your life when you were really grateful. It is a glorious feeling, a state of grace. Be willing to embrace all of your life experiences in gratitude knowing that they can be of value, especially the tough ones.

Expressing gratitude for your father can create a huge sense of freedom, especially at this time. Gratitude opens us to truly receiving the gifts we have been given. If your father is available, now would be a great time to express gratitude to him directly. Be willing to free yourself of past negative influences. A profound deepening of the relationship between father and son is possible during this time.

This provides another opportunity to use affirmations and clear the way for you to become more aware of the good in your life. "I am grateful for my father", "I am grateful for everything my father has given me", "I am grateful for my child". Just imagine how much you have to be grateful for. Be patient, breathe in between phrases and be creative with the process.

Through your inner preparation you can learn to integrate the gifts from your father, even if they did not have a lovely appearance or effect. If we are free of past influences and present to the joy in our lives now, more freedom is the inevitable result. We only need to awaken our awareness of it. This will prepare you well for the journey you have begun into fatherhood.

4

Beginning The Journey

Pregnancy

"What a father says to his children will not be heard by the world, but it will be heard for posterity."

Richter

For many men this time of becoming a father can lead to thoughts and feelings from a whole range of possibilities. They may include everything from excitement, to ambivalence, to panic. Important questions will also arise. What am I supposed to be doing? How will the baby affect my relationship with my partner? What about me? How can I get support for myself through all this?

Some men can find it difficult to ask for what they want or need. It can be easier, or more comfortable, to jump into the providing role and taking care of the needs of your partner. But you have your own legitimate needs. Meeting them will help you support your partner and your baby. First is getting in touch with what you need, then comes asking for it. If you are willing to invest some time in this the dividends will be great.

Following is an exercise that will help you identify your needs. Remember this is about what you need and want, not your partner or baby. Find somewhere comfortable where you can have a quiet moment. I invite you to write the answers to the following questions or close your eyes and contemplate them.

As a father what are you experiencing during this time? What kind of support do you need right now. What information or experience would help you to be more relaxed and present in your role? Do you need a confidant or mentor? How can you get support for yourself? What will allow you to engage more fully at this time and in the best way possible, for you? Relax, imagine and if you like, write about what it is that you need and want to support you as a father.

SexIntimacyRelationships

These three topics are so closely connected that they can seem as one. Almost any discussion about one will encompass aspects of another. These can also be among life's most exciting and fulfilling yet challenging issues. This period will certainly bring them into focus and present you with new opportunities for your personal development.

Sex

Sex is where this whole process started and it will be a central theme right the way through. Conception, giving birth and breastfeeding are all sexual experiences; they involve a woman's sexual anatomy. There are many dimensions of this to explore which could transform your experience of fatherhood.

A pregnant woman's body is a hormone factory, as well as a baby incubator. Her body produces biological cocktails which do wondrous things to support her and the baby's developing needs. One by-product is a shift to new and different priorities for her. Some of this is conscious; however, much of it is instinctual. Her attention has altered significantly from that of *being* a woman to include *becoming* a mother. Each woman will be individual in her experience and response.

This time can bring with it a new phase in a couple's sexual relationship. Some women will have an increase in their libido, others a reduction. If her sex drive is reduced it is important not to take this personally. It is not a statement about you or the importance of your relationship. Most importantly, it will change. During this time her physical, emotional and spiritual energy is focused on her baby. This may be more pronounced near the end of the pregnancy and for a time after the birth, particularly if she is breastfeeding. It is best for the two of you to speak about it regularly.

There are diverse cultural and spiritual beliefs and practices regarding this and it will vary as to how couples are with their sexual intimacy during this time. Some women feel inclined to abstain from sexual intercourse while pregnant. This may be an instinctual response for some. Certain spiritual practices recommend abstinence during the pregnancy as they feel the baby needs this space to be private and preserved for him alone. There are also cultures where the father is totally excluded from sexual contact during pregnancy and right the way through breastfeeding, for months or even years. What is most important is what works best for each couple. Also making love has many forms, penetration is just one of them, and this is generally safe throughout the pregnancy. Be gentle and allow your partner to guide you in what works best for her physical and emotional comfort. Speak about it.

If your sexual desire is higher than hers at this time acknowledge it, however, be conscious as to how you resolve it. Infidelity can appear to be a solution but rarely is a satisfying one in reality. It can also have long lasting consequences on your relationship and family. Also be aware of infidelities of the mind, which may not actually manifest physically. It is possible to redirect your sexual energy into another form of intimacy which you can all benefit from. If you find yourself straying, mentally or otherwise, work with your thoughts and find new ways to become closer to your partner and to express your love. Try a cuddle.

Just about every part of a woman's body can change during pregnancy. Some men are fine with this and others may be reticent about it. If you are in the second category, you may want to see if you can adjust your perception to one of acceptance. It is good to be honest with yourself; and use care if you speak with her about it. A woman's body image can be very sensitive during pregnancy and after the birth for a time.

Perhaps now may also be a good time to examine your personal views on women's bodies in general. The stereotypical 'body beautiful' standard that our culture exemplifies for women may deserve an adjustment. We have become prisoners to this image through advertising, film and other forms of commercial media. I think pregnant bodies are stunningly beautiful and a miracle of nature.

Using affirmations may support you.
"Change is safe" ,"I love my partner as she is",
"I am satisfied with my life".

Intimacy

Intimacy typically involves a close and loving connection between two people. Intimacy can be expressed and experienced in various ways; sex is only one of them. This time has the possibility to bring you and your partner closer together and provide you with a focal point for your love. Having a baby can be the most intimate and creative process two humans will ever know. Patience and the willingness to open your heart and trust the process will enhance your experience considerably.

A very important detail for men to know is that a woman's desire for intimacy, touching and holding is often increased during this time. Make an effort to tell her how special she is and how much she means to you. Express how much you appreciate who she is, as well as what she is doing through nurturing your child. What follows is one possibility.

Come together with your partner. Be sure you have the time and space to be alone and undisturbed. Make yourselves comfortable and sit facing each other. Gently, lovingly gaze into each others eyes. You may also want to lightly hold hands. Notice your breathing, perhaps even breath together; within the same cycle of in-breath and out-breath. Take the opportunity to 'fall in love' all over again. Notice this amazing and extraordinary person before you. Recall each other's qualities and attributes that attract you. Look deeply into each other's eyes and notice who is there, really there. You may also want to lie down and hold each other while eye gazing. You could do this regularly throughout the pregnancy. Working your way up to 20 minutes or more at a time would be great. A similar approach during labor can also be mutually supportive.

Remember she is your life partner, friend and lover. It is important to treat her as a woman, but not always as a pregnant woman. Of course connect with her belly, touch it, kiss it, and speak to your baby inside but individually acknowledge her. Pregnancy is a facet that has expanded who she is as a woman, but not the sum total of her parts. She, usually, does not want too much of her identity attached to her growing belly or the baby inside. An error many people make when communicating with a pregnant woman is that they relate to her belly first and foremost. The same principle applies once your baby is born. Mother and child are individuals. Acknowledge and recognize each of them, individually.

To me, love is an action verb. It is not just an emotional concept. It is an *expression AND demonstration* of how we feel (as opposed to just a feeling) and as such involves a type of doing. How many ways can you find to express your love to your family?

Some sample affirmations are: "I love my partner", "I welcome the changes that are happening", "I love being part of their intimacy and supporting it", "I am always included". Listen in and be gentle with yourself. What are your underlying thoughts and what new ones will better support everyone?

Relationships

Research, in the fields of science and psychology, has found that babies in the womb are aware of the experience they are having. They are also making complex decisions about these events. According to Dr. Yehudi Gordon, a UK pioneer of active and integrated birth healthcare, "During this period, your baby will learn more than in any other decade of her life. In the womb she hears noises and senses emotions."[6]

For each of us our time in the womb and early infancy was the beginning of our experience of intimacy and relationships. This is our original point of reference for relationships. We were in the center of our mother's world and we were experiencing life with and through her, physically and emotionally. Depending on how that was for you and your mother it could provide you with a fantastic model for your own relationships. If it had 'negative' elements it could also influence your own ability to form, keep or trust relationships. You may be compelled to leave or abandon relationships if that experience was dire in some ways. Decisions made regarding relationships, even ones from your preverbal time in the womb, can have an impact and be long lasting. And you can change them.

You may want to reflect on your own experience of relationships to see if you can identify any patterns you want to explore further. Memories of your time in the womb may seem inaccessible. However, you have access to your experience during that time through noticing how relationships have worked out for you, throughout your life. If there have been repeated patterns in your personal relationship history this may be a clue regarding earlier events and decisions you may have made. There are also numerous therapeutic approaches you could use for exploring and healing this.

A mother-to-be is growing a baby, inside of her body. Once she becomes pregnant there is an inner directed, non-stop process underway. As men we will never know just what being pregnant is like for a woman. However, what we can do is gather information and prepare ourselves, as best we can, so we can make the greatest possible contribution to our family. Welcome this opportunity to build on your relationship. Giving her regular massage is usually welcomed. This can be head, neck, shoulders, feet or whole body. Many women also place a high value on men doing things like projects around the house, things that will help prepare the home for the baby. This has actually been known to be a turn-on for some women.

You may think a father's physical experience came and went some time ago. Well not entirely. There are men who experience pregnancy symptoms of their own. Some fathers have hormonal changes and resulting emotional shifts. There are also those who have food sensitivities and cravings as well as lower back pain and weight gain. This is well documented and actually common. It is called the couvade. I suspect it is the result of the depth of connection between the parents and between a father and his child. There are also cultures where the father goes off to 'give birth' while the mother is in labor.

Reducing Stress

Life today can be full to overflowing with fast paced activities and demands on your time. In addition, your lack of familiarity with pregnancy, birth and fathering may evoke uncertainties, which can engender various fears. Stress can be the result. This is normal and there are a variety of ways you can assure your own wellbeing and that of your family.

Interestingly, the original use of the word stress was in relation to structural engineering. It denotes how much pressure or strain a piece of building material or a structure can withstand, before collapse. It is little wonder society uses the same word to apply to a human condition.

Stress can be compounded by *how you think*

about a situation or activity rather than just the actual thing itself. Perhaps, with the proper guidance and practice, you can avert some of the stress in the first instance.

Fear

Fear can come from thoughts about possible 'bad' outcomes of future events. Think about life: fear about money (I will not have enough), fear about safety (possible injury, birth), fear about time (there will not be enough), and fear about fathering (I will not be good enough). Without diminishing the importance of any of these concerns, it is valuable to notice they are all fears regarding the future. They are not 'real', in present time. We can have trepidation about what might happen. A very large percentage of what we tend to be concerned about never actually comes to pass. It is also these types of mental distractions that are likely to generate stress.

Fearful thoughts can also deprive us of experiencing the joy and satisfaction in whatever we are doing at any moment. In this way, we devalue our current activity. We miss part of the value by becoming distracted with the thoughts. It is important to remember that you have a choice about what you are thinking. Choose your thoughts with care. Remember to use the numerous tools and techniques presented throughout this book to support you in making helpful choices.

We often make decisions and hold beliefs from the past that we are not consciously aware of. If these were 'negative' in their impact on us, and left unresolved, they can add significant stress to our lives. There can be a contradiction between what we believe, reinforced by past experiences, and what we want now. This is especially true during important events or activities like relationships, birth and fathering.

My F2B colleague Elmer Postle wrote:

As we approach the subject of birth, we may notice feelings and bodily sensations arise. I was recently driving with a work colleague and our discussion landed on what we thought about birth. He said that every time he got into a conversation about birth he would notice his throat tightening, breathing speeding up and becoming flushed. It seemed our chatting in the car was touching the same sensations for him. I suggested it might be a memory from his own birth. He looked surprised though immediately said: "I was born by caesarean, they said I was too big to fit down the birth canal, I was a 'fat bastard'".

This was clear information to me about the nature of his birth. It was also accompanied by a sense of shame and wrongness and linked with how others held him responsible for the manner of his delivery. The symptoms he described suggested the issue was unresolved for him. In a few seconds the pace of our interaction was showing signs of speeding up considerably. I felt both blessed he had told me this about himself and concerned about properly dealing with the feelings that were arising. I told him that the feelings and sensations he reported were 'of interest to me and were significant'. The sense of emergency and the pace in our conversation then slowed down and we were able to pleasurably re-enter everyday conversation and finish our day's work.

I later asked myself: What unresolved story is he carrying towards becoming a father and the birth of any children he might ultimately have? What could truly be helpful? My simply saying, "yes, those could be relevant and accurate responses to something that happened at your birth", allowed another gentler option to be considered.

Begin to notice when your body and mind are giving you signals. Repetitive, fearful thoughts can compound each other and their effect on you. If you notice yourself clenching your fists, having a knot in your belly, fidgeting or your heart rate increasing then pause and take a few deep breaths. The 'activation' of these responses may be a result of experiences from your past. Current events can resurrect past traumas. Notice what the actual truth about a situation is. Is there a genuine reason to be afraid? Is there a real threat of some kind? If not, aim to restructure your view of an event or situation. Affirmations could be useful.

---

*"I am safe", "My partner is safe",
"My baby is safe".*

Time

Time is a key area people tend to stress over. Managing time can be a challenge when becoming a father. You may have many tasks and people wanting to have your attention, in addition to the requirements of your new role.

Two significant factors regarding time are how we think about it and how we priorities our use of it. Time has an illusionary quality to it. We each have twenty-four hours in a day to accomplish our lives, *and we do*. However, if we are not careful, we can fall into the trap of *thinking* that there is *not enough time*. How we think about it is important to our mental, emotional and physical wellbeing. Remind yourself regularly that you always have enough time to do what needs to get finished now.

There is a modern day concept called 'multitasking'. Perhaps this is a misnomer. Can we actually do more than one thing at a time? My computer can do several things at one time, if I tell it to, but I make the requests individually and sequentially. The very nature of this multi-tasking concept is perhaps indicative of modern society and how we view our relationship to time. We think that we *need* to do multiple things at the same time in order to accomplish what is *required* of us. Slow down; be with what you are doing now. Allow yourself to enjoy the task at hand.

At this point in your life prioritizing your use of time will become more important than ever. You will want to thoughtfully balance your work commitments with your new family ones. Speak with your partner about this and together do your best to get the balance that works for your family.

It is important to take the opportunity to engage with your new baby, while in the womb, and allow bonding to begin. You could get very close to your partner's belly and speak to your child. You might even speak so quietly that only your child can hear...it will be your little secret together. Acknowledge the relationship that already exists between you. This early period is precious and endearing. Take time off work if possible, a day or afternoon here and there, to be with your partner and your child. Take walks, hold each other and take time to connect. Speak about your new family and life together. Include your baby in these conversations.

Being Present

Another way we can become stressed is by doing one activity while thinking we *should* be doing something different. Being with your partner, while you are thinking that you should be working (or vice versa) will diminish the quality of your experience of both. If you are fully engaged in an activity it can be referred to as 'being present'. This is having your mind, body and emotions all engaged in the same activity.

We have all watched a sunset, danced a dance or been with our lover and had no other thoughts or concerns during that period; there was a timeless quality. These are typically the type of events during which we are fully present. You may notice there is no stress involved in such activities. You can expand your capacity for being present. Being with your partner in this way, truly present, is what each of you deserves.

———

Working with the following affirmations can be helpful. "I always have enough time", "I am enough, I do enough, I have enough", "I am always in the right place, at the right time, doing the right thing".

———

Breathing

Utilizing the breath can be a very useful for releasing and managing stress. The breath has the ability, when used with awareness, to positively influence your physical, mental and emotional wellbeing.

Physiologically, breathing is automatic; you do not have to think about it. This is similar to your heart beating; however breathing is also under your conscious control. In stressful situations you can alter your breathing to help you manage the energy in your body and still your mind and emotions. At peak times, for example during birth, if you notice you are breathing hard or fast you can consciously slow down your breath and you will begin to relax. Likewise, if you notice you are holding your breath, you can begin breathing, gently. Your mind and body will favorably respond by becoming more calm.

During a quiet time, observe your breath coming and going; give it a color or visual representation that works for you. Perhaps see your breath as a wheel, circular, so that the in-breath and the out-breath are continuous, flowing around or through your body. You can make use of your breath at any time and during any activity. Notice that by becoming aware of your breathing and creating a rhythm and pace with it you tend to be more peaceful.

There are also therapeutic uses for the breath which can be immensely valuable. Therapeutic Breathwork is guided by a practitioner/counselor. Various methods use conscious, intentional breathing to explore and release unconsciously held beliefs and emotional attachments to past experiences.[7]

Meditation

Meditation can be utilized by anyone in very simple forms. It could provide you with valuable support at this time. Find relaxing surroundings, a quiet place where you can be alone. Simply sit or lie down, make yourself comfortable and close your eyes. You could visualize a place where you feel relaxed if you like. This may be in a garden or by water. You might imagine a make-believe place or one you know. Allow yourself to go into deep relaxation. This may or may not come right away for you. With patience, the sensation will grow. Allow your thoughts to slow down and become fewer. During meditation it can also be useful to watch your breath and regulate it to enhance your experience.

Another option with meditation is to choose a word (known as a mantra) to help you to focus your attention. Find a word that represents something peaceful to you. Repeatedly and gently call the word to mind as you relax. This will help to draw your attention away from thoughts about the activities of life. Focusing a part of your mind on a mundane task, like repeating a word, allows the space for the rest of the mind to relax. Meditation will contribute significantly to your wellbeing.

It can also be mutually supportive to meditate with your partner. Sit quietly together, in silence. This is also a great time to get in touch with your baby. He is very receptive to contact with you.

You can practice for a few minutes here and there or, even better, 20 minutes twice a day. Relaxing music may be helpful or you may prefer silence. Choose what works for you. Any amount of practice is beneficial.

Father's Circle

The Father's Circle is another technique for creating calm. It will be particularly useful during the birth. Sit quietly with eyes closed and recall a time when you were at peace (imagine one if memory does not serve). Remember the circumstances and the feeling of peace you had. The more emotion you bring to the memory the better. Add whatever elements, colors or sensations which will make it more vivid for you. Really sense it.

Now, while holding that memory, firmly squeeze together your thumb and first finger on your right hand, forming a circle. This will cause a physical 'anchor' to link with that particular emotion. Keep your Father's Circle firmly intact while you replay your peaceful memory several times. Now do it again a few more times. The deeper you can go with this the better. Allow the calm feeling to flood through your mind and body. This may be quite subtle at first. Ultimately, when a stressful situation occurs, all you need do is form your Father's Circle and relaxation will set in. The physical anchor has been established.

If you like, you can take the Father's Circle for a test drive. Sit quietly with your fingers relaxed and apart. Recall a situation from the past which caused you some mild stress. Now, bring your fingers together to form your Father's Circle. Notice relaxation in your body and/or mind, however subtle. Imagine this situation being resolved peacefully. Practice this technique and allow the sensation of calm to build and become more pronounced. This is a tool that you can call on again and again when you notice yourself becoming stressed. Practice works.

5

Gifts For The Mother And Child

*"The most important thing that a father
can do for his children is to love their mother."*

Hesburgh

Following will be various additional suggestions of ways in which you can support your partner and child. Some are practical in nature and others are more experiential.

If you are a first time father you may feel unsure about exactly what your role is. Your partner's role is certainly obvious and she has the advantage of operating under the physical imperative that she is the one carrying the baby. Your baby's role is not in question either and may seem effortless and automatic. What if there is something special that your family needs and you are the only one who can provide it? Would you want to know what it is?

Empathy and understanding are invaluable here. Understanding others and their unique experience of life can go a long way towards helping you know how to best support them. Following is an exercise in empathy. You will be guided to imagine yourself in the role of a mother and a baby during the time of pregnancy. As you do this notice your thoughts, feelings and sensations in your body. These are feedback mechanisms which you can learn from.

Empathy Exercise:
A baby during pregnancy

Imagine that you are a baby in the womb, very small and in a constant state of growth. What can you picture that you want for yourself while in the womb? Remember that the baby is present for everything the mother experiences: hears, thinks, feels and does. What would you want your parents' relationship to be like? What kind of input would you like from your father? What is important to you? Remember things like sounds, nourishment, physical awareness, emotional environment, people and more. Consider this time, as a baby develops physically, mentally and emotionally over these months.

Sit back, close your eyes and imagine being a baby, growing inside a womb. It is your choice as to how you work with these suggestions. You may want to just imagine your responses or write them out. These explorations may take you deeper than you had imagined. Be gentle with yourself and get support if you need it.

A woman during pregnancy

Now imagine you are a pregnant woman. You are feeling emotions as never before. You may be experiencing doubts and fears, joys and elation. It can seem as if your body and mind are being taken over by someone or something else. Your body is changing externally as well from being a woman to also include being a mother. How do you feel about these changes? What supports you to be able to do the job at hand as well as still manage your life and relationships? What kind of support would you like to have from the father? What is it like to be in such close contact with another?

Sit back and really imagine what this would be like. What do you need and want during this most extraordinary time? Imagine you are a pregnant woman and you have a baby growing inside of you.

Morning Wellness

In 1980 my then wife, Kathryn, and I were on vacation in Hawaii. She began waking in the mornings with nausea, although otherwise healthy. We had been eagerly working on having a second child. After a couple of days, reality dawned and we became aware she was pregnant. We were thrilled, but the nausea persisted. We wondered about dealing with the nausea using affirmations. We wanted to explore the nausea as a possible psychosomatic response to the pregnancy. Was there a conflict between her conscious and unconscious thoughts about having another child?

We already understood that a possible emotional component to nausea had to do with 'digesting new ideas'. We knew this from working with the book <u>Heal Your Body</u>, by Louise Hay.[8] We were experienced with affirmations and their value in changing long held beliefs. However, we had never tried using affirmations in order to resolve so immediate an issue like nausea. We were curious just how much influence they could have.

Kathryn put pen and paper next to the bed and when she awoke the next morning, with nausea, she began writing. She wrote an affirmation and then paused and listened in to see if she had a harmonious internal response, or not. Her writing was an exploration of her thoughts, feelings and beliefs; not just the inputting of words or phrases. She wrote that she was happy about the pregnancy; her response was not an enthusiastic yes. She wrote that this was the perfect time to get pregnant; she discovered inner conflict. She also uncovered residual fear, based on the possibility of repeating the traumatic experience of giving birth to our first child. She wrote that she really wanted another child now; however discovered hesitation.

Keep in mind that Kathryn wanted another child and yet for her there were previously unresolved issues at work, unconsciously. Over the next few days she repeated this process first thing in the morning. Each day the nausea was less intense and dissipated more quickly. By the fourth day she awoke completely at ease and welcoming our new child.

I have recommended this technique to many mothers since 1980 and they have reported a very high rate of success and subsequently expressed much gratitude. This is one of many examples of how what we think, even though we are unaware of the thoughts, can have an effect in our lives. There can also be physiological components inherent in what is called morning sickness. This is not to say that affirmations will be effective for everyone or that they are to be considered a cure, but certainly worth a try.

Midwives and Birth Coaches

The people who will support you during the birth are important and are best when in alignment with yours and your partner's wishes. This includes healthcare professionals. It is key to have support from people who have confidence in the fundamental healthiness of birth and the capability of a woman to carry it out. Know who you are inviting into your family experience, if at all possible. In a hospital setting this may be a challenge. However do what you can and consciously assert yourself to achieve the best results possible.

There is great value in having your own dedicated midwife, especially one who understands the inherent safety of birth. The type of committed support they can provide is profound. Another very real value is the continuity of care that you receive by having the same professional with you throughout the labor and birth. The birth of this child will be a one time only experience for you, your partner and especially your child. You all deserve the most loving and supportive people and environment possible. Only accept what feels right to the two of you. This is your family's birth.

A professional birth coach (also known as a doula) is a trained birth attendant. She is dedicated to you and trained in supporting your family during the birthing time. She can be a very valuable asset to you and your partner. She can also free you up to be the loving support person for your partner rather than the one expected to be a coach or a birth professional. If you can be freed up to do just the loving support I highly recommend it. You could have an private midwife and/or birth coach with you at home or in the hospital.

There are usually extra financial costs involved in having a private midwife or doula.

Some people are perplexed as to why they should spend extra money on a birth when a service is already provided, typically by your insurance company. Have you spent money on a wedding, house, vacation or car? Were you careful about planning and being sure you got what you really wanted for these items or events? Did you consider the short term and long term value or return on investment for them? Although birth may seem like a brief moment in time the impact is lasting and paramount for your child. Your family deserves the best support you can afford.

Also consider having male support to back you up. He would probably not be in the birthing room, but nearby. You may need a break, someone to talk to or to get something you may need. He could sit at the door or just be available by phone to provide reassurance for you. This alone can be very valuable. You will be in a very strong supporting role and you need support as well.

Listening and Fixing

A pregnant woman is under the influence of spectacular hormones day and night. These hormones, more likely than not, will cause her to experience deep emotions more frequently. A man, typically, wants to immediately fix whatever is not to a woman's liking. Many men have what I call the 'fixing gene'. It has not been proved yet by science, however the anecdotal evidence is overwhelming. Fixing is not necessarily what is always called for however.

A friend of mine, Peter, was with his partner who was very upset. She began to rant, which was not uncommon for her. Peter did something out of the ordinary for him, he listened. He did not speak. He nodded his head in response to specific points she made. He made sincere sounds that indicated he understood what she was going through, yet he used no words. He did not take anything she said personally, even though some of it was aimed directly at him. He also did not try to defend himself. He resisted the temptation to try to make her feel better, fix it for her, or do anything. Peter told me that what followed was some of the best sex they had had in months.

There is a clue here, rather than the outcome being a coincidence. Women place a high value on being listened to. We all want to feel that we are being heard. This doubles for a woman and quadruples for a pregnant woman. This is what I call simple math. Being heard is a significant aspect of intimacy for women. They will feel closer to you as a result. They feel accepted and valued; they relax and feel safer. We all do actually.

Listen for the words, "Will you please fix XYZ",

or "Would you do something about XYZ". If you do not hear these or similar words the chances are that fixing is not what she wants or needs as an outcome. Pause, take a breath and listen.

A Fathers-To-Be participant of ours and his partner have established a once a week 'talking stick' time. They realized they were getting carried away with all of the intensity of life and the pregnancy and were not connecting in a way that was satisfying for them. They plan a specific time to have an intentional conversation and connect with each other on more than just daily activities. A stick, or other convenient object, is passed back and forth and used to designate whose turn it is to speak. The other person listens and says nothing. This practice comes from Native American tradition. They established this during the pregnancy and were still using it almost a year later. They find it continues to support their relationship.

Lightening Up

The sheer volume of new experiences during this time can become overwhelming if you let them. Instead you can address some events and situations with wonder and wit. Be willing to discover the humor in what is happening. Find ways to make your partner laugh. Laughter can shift emotional energy better than anything else and there may be a time or two that movement is what is called for.

Anyone who has ever seen the naked profile of a woman who is nine months pregnant has got to be amazed at the capacity of the female body to change. No other living thing on this planet displays this. What about those breasts? Her cup size multiplies in a matter of weeks. And just wait until you see them shoot milk across the room. And the baby, well, the phrase 'bodily functions' will soon take on a whole new connotation. You are going to have a front row seat and a leading role. Enjoy the process.

Acceptance

A woman, during the birthing time, has a particular job to do. She is being driven by many physiological and emotional elements. As a gift to your family, consider practicing unconditional acceptance of your partner. Practically, this means accepting her and all of her actions. In other words, suspend all judgments. Say yes (at least silently) to her state of mind, body and emotions. Be willing to listen to whining, body symptoms, emotional issues and complaints about you and the rest of the world. This does not mean you agree with her on everything but that you accept her and the experience she is having. Avoid arguments if possible. Attempt to not take things personally, especially during labor. Take a few deep breaths before responding, especially if she has a go at you. Being right, and winning arguments in relationships, is way overrated. This practice will also contribute to your child's wellbeing significantly. Your partner will produce fewer stress hormones and will be more relaxed and as a result the baby's environment will be as well.

Bruce Lipton, Ph.D. explains it scientifically:

"During pregnancy, the parent's perception of the environment is chemically communicated to the fetus through the placenta, the cellular barrier between the maternal and fetal blood. The mother's blood-borne emotional chemicals cross the placenta and affect the same target cells in the fetus as those in the parent. Though the developing child is "unaware" of the details (i.e., the stories) evoking the mother's emotional response, they are aware of the emotion's physiological consequences and sensations. While developing in the safety and confinement of the uterus, the child is provided a preview of the environment as it is defined by the parent's perception and behavior. Parental behaviors' are generally cyclic, and when repeated, they serve to habituate the developing behavioral chemistry in the fetus. Consequently, parental perceptions and responses to environmental stress are imparted to the offspring and serve in programming its behavioral expression."[9]

This is not to say that every moment of a pregnancy needs to be perfect or that damage will occur if it is otherwise. Emotional honesty and expression is healthy. Raising emotional issues that need to be cleared is very important, as you are learning throughout this book. However, repetitive and sustained states of emotional or physical stress can have a compounded effect on your baby. This is similar to adults, except babies are more vulnerable.

To accomplish acceptance, to whatever degree you can, is a profound undertaking. The by-product is tremendous freedom for both of you. When you stop the mental chatter about others and allow them to be as they are you gain great benefit. Accept her, accept yourself, and accept a new level of inner peace.

Welcome

Welcome is a profound greeting. Recall how you have felt when someone said "Welcome" to you, and really meant it. World-wide, various rituals are practiced within tribes, cultures and families to demonstrate welcome to a new child and the parents. One common western tradition is having a baby shower. There are other cultures where a ceremony is performed to welcome a child before conception. He is welcomed again once pregnancy occurs and, of course, once the he is born. Imagine what it would be like to be told you are welcome and to always feel welcome. My wife's grandfather bought her a pony and commissioned a customized pony saddle for her when her arrival was announced. They lived in Texas. This was his way of expressing his welcome. How would you like to welcome and invite your child into your family? Perhaps create your own ritual, or borrow one. Following is a lovely alternative for demonstrating welcome, written by Laura Uplinger and Jack Bresnahan.

Threesome

Within an intimacy, take your hands
and hold them to your partner's pregnant belly.
With the three of you gathered together,
have a conversation about this family.
Talk about who you are.
About your home, your life, ideas, hopes, dreams.
"Your mom and I were picturing your
first taste of chocolate ice cream."
"Your dad wants to take you sailing."
"Welcome to this tough old world.
You will make a difference."
"What a joy you are! We're honored to be yours."
"Count on us."
Then give all three of you a deep felt family kiss.

6

Preparing For Birth

*"The greatest use of a life is to
spend it on something that will outlast it."*

William James

I have found being at births profoundly rewarding. Birth is, however, a female event and a very personal time for a woman. She needs to feel safe and supported, whatever that means for her. She may want to be at home, in a birth center or in hospital; alone (known as Unassisted Birth[10]) or just with a midwife; in water, moving around or squatting. As is most often the case today, she will likely want you included and very involved in supporting her. Her wishes may also change several times during her pregnancy or labor, which is her right. Your job is to be of service to her and your baby. If she wants you at the birth, and you wish to participate, then you are privileged indeed. Discuss what role you will provide. Most of all, regard it as though you have been invited to a fabulous banquet. It is a banquet celebrating life and love. You, the mother and baby are the guests of honor.

Managing Your Energy

Learning to manage your thoughts, emotions and physical energy is invaluable. It will better prepare you to handle the many new experiences that you will be presented with during this time, especially at the birth. There will also be direct benefits for your family.

Oxytocin is a hormone a woman's body produces. It is a necessary element for the onset and progress of labor and the birth. However, if adrenalin is present in the woman's body it will cancel out oxytocin and labor can slow down or even stop. Adrenalin production can be a direct neuro-chemical response to fear or anxiety. In addition, adrenalin can be transferred across distance, from person to person; it is 'contagious'. Can you recall a time when someone near you was anxious or angry and just their presence unsettled you and caused you anxiety as well? This is the same response mechanism that can affect a laboring woman. The mother can be affected if you or anyone else near her is wound up or afraid. You can learn to manage your physical and emotional energy and remain calm. This will be something of value you can *provide for* your partner and child.

Lars, a father of two, related a story to me about the pending birth of his third child. *"I was away on a business trip when my wife, Jiaya, called to report that she was having contractions. When I arrived home she was well into her labor and thrilled that I was there. However, it soon became apparent we were having a challenge connecting. I was still in 'business mode'. I was not really present yet. Jiaya became distracted and agitated because of the dissimilarity between us. I could tell her stress level was becoming elevated as a result. Jiaya's labor slowed down and subsequently came to a complete halt."*

Fortunately, because of the preparation they had done, they knew what to do. They paused and had a lie down together. They held each other and looked into each others eyes; they started a gentle breathing cycle together. This encompassed a couple of hours, there was no hurry. Jiaya told me, *"As we connected I could feel Lars 'land'. I began to feel safe in his presence, in his arms, in his love. I surrendered fully and as I did, after awhile, my contractions began again."* Jiaya's body and mind relaxed when she felt she and Lars were in harmony. They were in connection and doing it together.

A woman, who trusts and feels safe and intimate with her partner, can more easily open up and let go. Their son, Noah, was born a few hours later. Fathers are important and they make a difference at birth. Even though they are not the ones giving birth, the nature of their presence can have a considerable effect on the labor and birth.

Begin noticing your body: when you tighten up, clench your jaw or fists or get a knot in your belly. These are all indicators of nervousness, anxiety or fear. We all experience this now and then, especially with first time occurrences like birth. When this happens, notice

your thoughts also. There is usually a correlation between what you are thinking and how
your body and emotions are responding. This
level of attention may necessitate some practice if it is new to you. Learning to attune to
your own personal anxiety responses will
prove very valuable. Meditation, visualization,
breathing, the Father's Circle and affirmations
will all support you as well. Any level of self-
awareness is good and you can practice to get
better. Perhaps also practice with your partner. Physical exercise can also help you to reduce your stress levels.

Calm is a quality that deserves to be empha-
sized. If a father has low stress levels and a
quiet mind, what remains is calmness. This is
a most valuable contribution and exactly what
the mother needs. It is a bit like being a sculp-
tor. When viewing a sculpture the work that
has been done to create it is not visible. It is
the space around the sculpture that gives it
form and purpose. Like the space you are now
providing, around your family. What you have
done is remove mental chatter and fearful
thoughts and what remains is calm. Consider
yourself an artist and you are sculpting an environment where your family can be held in
your tranquility and love.

Another way to deal with stress and reduce
adrenalin is through repetitive motions. Using
a stress release ball (a rubber ball that fits

into the palm of your hand) is a good example. Squeezing the ball re-directs physical energy and dissipates it. One of these comes in the Fathers-To-Be Tool Kit. Similarly, a midwife 'in the know' will sometimes knit or read during a woman's labor. Her awareness is still with the mother yet she is directing her physical energy through another activity and letting the woman progress without too much attention on her.

My Preparation for a Birth

My preparation for my second child's water-birth was wide-ranging. My wife and I had counseling, individually and together. We wanted to resolve any concerns or fears we had about birth in general or the use of water. In the end, we reached certainty about both.

It was 1980 and ours was the first docu-mented waterbirth in the US so there were no books to read or Google to search for what to do and how. We brought together a few friends and colleagues and held several meetings to prepare everyone. We interviewed numerous doctors and midwives. They all wanted to be as far away from the event as possible except for one midwife, whom we employed.

I rented a portable, fiberglass Jacuzzi and had 300 gallons of distilled water delivered (a bit over the top, but who knew?). Next, I transformed our two car garage into a functional and beautiful waterbirth room. Using my carpentry skills I built a wood frame bed platform next to the tub. This was in case Kathryn decided she wanted to give birth outside the water. I hung pictures and curtains on the walls to make it cozy and placed oriental rugs on the floor. We had motion and still camera's standing by to record this historic event. I filled the tub and heated the water.

Kathryn's labor began suddenly and progressed quickly. She was feeling overwhelmed by the intensity of her contractions. Kathryn and I entered the wondrous and almost mystical atmosphere we had created; to welcome our child. As we immersed ourselves in the water we were enveloped by its' warmth. Kathryn was relieved by the comfort and freedom of movement the water afforded her. The support team arrived at various times and quietly assumed their roles. After only a ninety minute labor Kathryn birthed Jeremy into my willing hands. For a few minutes Jeremy was suspended in his expanded watery world peacefully integrating his experience, time stood still. I felt privileged, humble and proud; all in an instant. The three of us embraced.

We had a sense that the inner preparation we had done was central to our experience. We were unencumbered and available for every aspect of the birth of our child. We felt like we had participated in a miracle, and we had.

7

Empowered Birth

"Fathers, like mothers, are not born.
Men grow into fathers - and fathering is
a very important stage in their development."

David M. Gottesman

Birth is the most profound act of love imaginable. It is also a rite of passage for a child as well as the parents. From ancient caves and huts to modern homes and hospitals birth has been, and always will be, a very primal event and an initiation for everyone involved. Neither weight lifters nor marathon runners can hold a candle to the strength and fortitude demonstrated by a mother when birthing her child. For a father the experience is distinctly different yet can be equally profound.

During labor stay close to your partner. With my first child's birth I was in eye to eye contact with his mother virtually the entire time. Praise her, encourage her and let her know what a wonderful job she is doing. A woman can receive tremendous support through your full presence. She will feel more like she is sharing her labor with you. Assuming this is in harmony with what she wants. Take your clues from her as to what kind of support she wants and how. Listen. Her desires are also likely to change throughout the labor. Less talking is usually better than too much. I encourage you to be involved as much as possible, all the way to catching your child when he is born. You will be glad you did.

Empathy Exercise:
A baby during birth

Imagine you are a baby in the womb and it is nine months since you were conceived. As your hormone activity accelerates you are experiencing changes inside your body. You also notice pressure from the sides of the only home you have known. It is time for a big transition: birth. How is this for you? How would you like the outside environment to be for your arrival? Who do you want to be there to greet you? How do you want to be handled? What about interventions in the process? As soon as you are born, where do you want to be and with whom?

Imagine how you would want to be received and treated by those around you during this most intense and significant time? What is important to you? What do you need? Visualize it or write about it.

A woman during birth

Imagine you are in labor and about to give birth? What do you think the nature of your journey will be like? What kind of support will be best for you? This includes the people you want with you and the environment you will be in. Most of your attention is being focused in your lower body. Your mental and emotional processes are significantly altered due to the hormones that have come to support the birth. Your body has taken over and the energy of birth is commanding your full attention. What role would you want your partner to play?

Imagine what you would do with all of this energy in your body. How you would handle it? What would make it as wonderful as possible for you? Feel free to imagine it or write about it.

Pain Relief

Fathers can be afraid for their partners. Many, including my son Anandas, have told me if they could they would gladly take on the pain for her. Now, where would fathers get the idea that pain is involved in birth if they have never actually seen one? The first possibility would be their own birth experience, when they were born. Evidence shows that babies are conscious before and at birth and they do remember their experience, including pain, although not necessarily consciously.

David Chamberlain writes in his book <u>The Mind of Your Newborn Baby</u>: "The truth is, much of what we have traditionally believed about babies is false. They are not simple beings but complex and ageless small creatures with unexpectedly large thoughts."[11]

The second possibility, regarding birth being painful, is virtually every cultural and societal reference to birth we have all been exposed to our entire lives. From family stories to the bible, television and films, childbirth is represented as excruciating. It is little wonder most people believe pain is inevitable in birth. However, many women also experience pleasure.

While you cannot literally take away pain, you can be a significant contributor to your partner's *less painful* and therefore more joyful experience of birth. You can help provide the kind of environment and support that will have the greatest possibility to allow her what she needs to be instinctual and inner directed in her birthing. It is also helpful to watch films together of satisfying, fulfilling births during the pregnancy. Watch the film Orgasmic Birth.

In the mid-twentieth century Dr. Robert A. Bradley, a US obstetrician, began integrating fathers into labor and birth. Over his career he presided over twenty thousand births with fathers present. Ninety percent were totally unmedicated. He found that the father's presence supported the mother to be more relaxed. His approach revolved around praise, encouragement and assurance of progress. The doctor was in the background, 'like a lifeguard at a swimming pool'.[12]

YES! Birth

Many women have a pain-free birth experience. YES, they feel the energy of the labor. YES, they feel big surges in their body. If a woman can say YES to everything she is feeling, and work with the tremendous energy, transformation can occur in her mind and body. If a woman can welcome this profound energy she can expand with it. You can support your laboring partner by reminding her that she can do it, that she is safe and to say YES. Her hormones will respond to YES also.

Even if there is pain the best approach is to work with the pain. Resistance can cause more pain. Resistance is saying NO and holding on. Let the pain happen. Surrendering to the pain is letting go and this can allow it to transform and lessen in intensity. Say YES, literally and out loud. The possibility exists for her to open her mind and relax her body and receive her baby in a wholly satisfying and empowering way; even in pleasure. It happens and it typically happens with women who hold a positive view of birth. Also remember to say YES yourself to everything you experience during the birth. Let YES become part of the pregnancy, the birth and your life.

Dr. Grantly Dick-Read, an English physician, explained it in this way: "When a woman is in a state of fear, messages are sent to the body telling it there is a danger out there that must be fought or run away from. Blood and oxygen are instantly sent into the arms and legs enabling the frightened woman to fight the danger or run away. In order for this to happen, however, blood and oxygen must be drained from other organs which the body considers nonessential for fight or flight."

Unfortunately, when it comes to fight or flight, the uterus is considered a nonessential organ. Hence, the laboring woman experiences not only pain, but a multitude of problems. The solution, he believed, was twofold: "Not only do women need to stop being afraid, but doctors need to stop interfering in the process. Laboring women do not need to be poked, prodded, and drugged. Instead, they need to be calmly encouraged, or simply left alone so their bodies may work unhindered".[13]

Environment

I recommend a birth environment as calm, lovely, natural, familiar and as comfortable as possible. This description fits almost any home. Except when there is an actual medical condition, fear is the most common barrier to birthing at home. This is understandable, based on society's long standing view of birth as dangerous. It is possible to dispel fears and be free to make a choice based on where and how a family wants their birth. At the end of the day, what is most important is that a birthing woman feels safe, wherever she is. Do your research and education, become informed together, and then fully support her choice. There are additional resources listed in the back of this book to support you.

The waterbirth room I created for my second child's birth is perhaps the furthest degree of physical preparation and environment by design. As a father it became part of my ritual in preparation for the birth. It was one of my ways of welcoming my child. Of course, it was also a way of providing something of value for my wife.

Using a water pool for the labor and birth is perhaps the most physically supportive option. It provides freedom of movement, warmth and comfort for the mother. The baby also has the possibility for a sense of continuity; from the warm, moist and mostly gravity-free womb environment, to the outside into similar surroundings. Receiving my son Jeremy in this way was lovely to behold and be part of. Waterbirth is not, however, always available or desired. Homebirth, under the right circumstances, has been proved to be very safe, safer than hospital birth actually.

Creating an environment of your choosing can

be more of a challenge if you are going to be in a hospital. However, you can still have an influence. Bring some things from home that will provide familiarity and comfort for both of you. Also cover or remove distracting items.

In his book, <u>Magical Child</u>, Joseph Chilton Pearce says, "Intelligence grows by moving from the known to the unknown and referring back to the known. No new experience can be accepted and interpreted unless it has at least some similarity to past experience."[14]

One cannot gain intelligence and defend oneself at the same time. This pertains to all of us but especially babies at birth as they are in an accelerated process of brain development. Birth is a significant transition and journey into the unknown for this highly aware and sensitive young person. The more reference points of familiarity a baby has, during and after birth, the better. Unfamiliarity, pain and separation all activate survival/defense mechanisms and stress hormones. Familiarity provides continuity.

Birth and Sex

The birth itself is also an aspect of sexual experience, and even expression for some. When a woman gives birth, her body and sexual anatomy is involved and highly exposed. As the birth draws nearer, this reality can be confronting for mothers and fathers. Your partner is going to reveal herself in a very big way, physically and emotionally, and probably in front of total strangers if you are to be at a hospital. This level of intimacy had previously been reserved for just the two of you, in total privacy. Your reaction to this may surprise you. This is rarely talked about. It is good to speak about this in advance with your partner in order to support each other. Also, some women do not want their partners to see 'down there' when they are giving birth. They think it may put them off sex with them in the future. If your partner has specific requests that will make her more comfortable talk about it, and do what you can to support her.

According to natural birth proponent Sheila Kitzinger, a similar environment to the one you and your partner conceived your baby in is ideal for giving birth. Perhaps it was quiet, calm, lovely and intimate. There are couples who make love to kick-start labor. Some make love during labor and utilize nipple and clitoral stimulation. There is hard science that shows that this can have significant benefits for the laboring woman. Oxytocin is produced when a woman is sexually stirred. It is one of the hormones that encourage the onset and progression of labor, as well as pain relief. Oxytocin has been called the "hormone of love". The same hormone that got the baby in there is also the one that will help the baby come out.

Also, the vagina opens more when stimulated. Taking this even further, semen contains prostaglandin, a hormone that helps the cervix (the entry to the birth canal) to open.

Some women choose to perceive and feel birth as a sensual experience, and go all the way with that feeling. There are also women who have a spontaneous, and often unexpected, orgasm during birth. Certain conditions are typically a prerequisite for this to happen. These include a sense of safety, trust, intimacy and the ability to let go and relax. If a woman feels nurtured and uninhibited an ecstatic state is possible. The science is there. What if the passion, privacy and support were also? Explore the DVD Ecstatic Birth.[15]

Support or Interference

The unnecessary use of *any drugs* or the utilization of *mechanical or medical procedures* during birth can begin a cascade toward more and more intervention. In other words, intervention can cause complications. If a laboring woman's natural progression of biological events has been disturbed, each subsequent stage is affected and can become disabled as a result. The ultimate intervention is a caesarean section. In this operation a doctor cuts into the mother's abdomen and removes the baby. A caesarean is major surgery and as such has risks; significantly more so than normal vaginal deliveries. A caesarean is an excellent rescue operation, *when absolutely necessary.* Medical support, under the right circumstances, is invaluable and important, and is best when its use is measured.

The 'fixing gene' can reveal itself during birth. If you are in a hospital you will be in an unfamiliar environment and this alone can cause insecurities and fears. Hospital routines are based on a fixing model, so be aware. This will be a peak experience, emotions will be running high and you and your partner will be in unfamiliar surroundings and very vulnerable. Inform yourself in advance of your obstetrician's and hospital's policies and procedures regarding 'managing births'. The mother should be respected and empowered to carry out her labor as she feels to. Have a personal birth plan, stating what you both want, and make sure the hospital staff has a copy, is familiar with it and above all agree to it.

Being active during labor is usually best for a woman. Freedom of movement gives a woman the choice to be in whatever position works for her body. Moving her body helps the baby move as well. Gravity will also be a useful asset which only applies if the woman is standing, squatting or kneeling, certainly not on her back. Being horizontal is usually the least helpful position. Think about it.

A woman's body is perfectly designed to give birth. Except in a small number of situations, a normal, natural birth is possible. Consider informing the staff that requests for interventions are to be brought to you first. This can allow your partner space for what she needs to do. If intervention of any kind is proposed, ask for evidence that it is necessary, what options there may be, and what the possible outcomes are if there is no intervention. It can be supportive, if faced with a decision, to ask for a few minutes to consider a response. Discuss options with your partner, in-between contractions not during one. Consider, with your partner, what your options are and what you want. Birth is rarely an emergency situation, although it may seem the opposite because it is so intense. Come from calmness, avoid reacting.

Dr. Thomas Verny puts forth two 'laws' regarding a labor room environment.
First: *The quantity of technological devices in the labor room is inversely proportional to the amount of human contact between staff and patient.*
Second: *The quantity of technological devices in the labor room is directly related to the degree of discomfort experienced by the patient.*[16]

Today's society tends to focus mostly on the outward, physical outcome of birth. That is to say, on the body. Perhaps because of this the caesarean is often being used as defensive medicine. If the mother and baby survive, the birth is a success. Parents can easily fall under this illusion. They do not want to risk the safety of the baby or the mother. This is certainly understandable. Because of their limited birth physiology and medical knowledge they are depending on the professionals for guidance. They can also be eager to be finished with the drama of the birth and overjoyed at the prospect of holding their new baby. However, what do we sacrifice and what are the resulting costs, in human terms?

We would all do well to consider the entire person – body, mind, emotions and spirit. We could then, perhaps, comprehend the total impact of birth on the wellbeing of the child the parents and society. The mind and body possess an autobiography of the whole self. They tell us the story of the life and times of a person, from conception onward, stored in their cells. This story then becomes a filter through which an individual perceives, interprets and experiences life. Through the care of our children, from the start, we can add precious value to their lives.

Umbilical Cord

Leaving the umbilical cord intact after birth is important. A habit had developed in modern culture of immediately clamping/cutting the cord and then hanging the newborn by their ankles and slapping their bottom to get them to breathe right away. This has changed to some degree but cutting the cord immediately is still common. The cord circulates blood between the placenta and the baby. The blood delivers nutrients to the baby, especially oxygen. Our need for oxygen is continuous, moment to moment. If the cord is immediately cut the baby will have no source of oxygen and panic will ensue. Survival mechanisms will kick in and stress hormones will flood their body. Your baby can feel like he is in a life and death situation, physically and emotionally. Many of us have had experiences, perhaps when swimming, when we were at risk of being oxygen deprived. How did it feel?

The cord, together with the placenta, contains as much as 30% of the potential blood supply for the baby. Cutting the cord too early will deprive the baby of a significant amount of this blood. Early cutting can also reduce the red blood cell count and therefore the effectiveness of the baby's immune system. Delayed cutting of the cord will enhance blood supply, enrich iron stores, reduce the risk of anemia and cut in half the risk of serious blood disorders.[17]

The cord is also the baby's physical connection with the mother and familiarity. It is important for continuity, bonding and brain development. What are we teaching this receptive new baby? If the cord is left connected the baby will breathe in his own time, gently and naturally, to his own rhythm. It will not always look like a big gasp, a scream and a struggle.

It is common medical practice to immediately cut the cord and give the mother an injection of artificial hormones to cause the placenta to detach. The placenta will usually detach naturally, if allowed to. It will take a bit longer than if drugs are used. You have all the time in the world. It is actually best to leave the umbilical cord connected until after the placenta delivers. At that point the baby is complete with this phase of life. The mother's and baby's bodies have told us so, because the placenta has delivered. Again, non-intervention allows nature to take its intended course. Ask your healthcare provider for what you want for your family.

David Chamberlain underlines this in Elmer Postle's documentary film, <u>The Healing of Birth, Invitation to Intimacy</u>. He refers to babies screaming as a reaction to their treatment at birth, "We used to say, what a healthy baby. Well, we were not treating that as genuine communication."[18] There is, typically, some stress involved in birth, as distinct from trauma. A moderate amount of stress is not necessarily a bad thing. Compounded trauma however can have lasting effects and may be able to be avoided in many instances.

Family Bonding

The minutes immediately after your baby is born are precious. You will likely remember them forever. Your child will as well, at a very deep level. This is the primary bonding time for your family and is paramount. Do what you can to ensure this process is as comfortable and supported as possible. Your baby is best placed immediately on your partner's tummy/chest; cord still intact with direct skin to skin contact. This is what nature intended and wants. Unnecessary separation can have lasting effects. Your baby has already undergone parting from his mother's body, the home he knew, and needs as many elements of familiarity as possible.

Unless there is an actual and immediate medical emergency, accept nothing less than continuous connection between mother and baby. Everything else can wait. Cleaning and poking and weighing and all of the common procedures are secondary to your family's initial time together. Also be sure to speak to your new baby. He will recognize your voice and it will add comfort and familiarity. Also, close eye to eye contact is important for all three of you. If there is a very good reason to separate mother and baby then you are the next best one to be with your child. Keep him in connection with you if this happens, if at all possible.

Debriefing after Birth

There are different layers of possibility with debriefing after a birth. I recommend debriefing for everyone involved in every birth. Writing about your experience of the birth can be very valuable. This writing is for you and not necessarily to share with anyone. Writing is one type of debriefing and you may also want to speak with someone. You and your partner would do well to speak together about your individual experiences. Express what the birth was like for you. How did you feel? Perhaps describe it physically as a framework to access the deeper stuff. Speaking with another father may be good for you too; if it is someone who is sensitive and you can open to. You could also speak with your own father. And you may also want to speak with a counselor.

I have worked with new fathers in this way and they have found it to be of profound value. Debriefing is also valuable with birth experiences from years ago. This will support the birth of subsequent children you may have. Without debriefing or resolution of some kind these peak experiences can sort of rattle around inside and become a distraction from the love that is present to experience. The important thing is that you feel complete and whole.

You can also tell the birth story to your new baby. They may be pre-verbal however they have an intelligence and understanding that is real, for them. Any time we have a significant experience in life it is valuable to acknowledge it and how it was for us. This allows integration. The same is true for your baby.

Integrating the Outcome of Birth

Every birth is different and will be a unique experience for each person present. It could be a glorious experience and you will bask in its' glow for years to come. However, the birth of your child could turn out differently than you planned. There may be unexpected or adverse aspects to it. This can be a challenge to integrate and accept. Because of the very personal nature of birth there is often an element of mourning involved in a birth that did not go to plan.

Over several decades of working directly with birth, as well as with adults in the therapeutic realm, I have learned that every birth has something to teach us. This is not to say that it was all a brilliant experience for you or your baby and partner, on the surface. Once it is over however, it is an experience in the past.

Get support for yourself if you need it. Give yourself permission to cry or be angry (in a safe way) and express exactly how you feel. This is an important part of the process.

Then, give thanks and do your best to accept the birth. Allow yourselves the space to learn from it and heal. The traumatic birth of my first child is an example. It stimulated me to explore myself and research and then to develop waterbirth. Subsequently, the combination of the two births and life experience led me to my current work with fathers and childbirth professionals. I am deeply grateful for all of it.

The birth of your child will be an initiation into an entirely new phase of your life. It is a pivotal point in your transition to fatherhood. Take as much time as possible to be with your new family. Partake in every sensation. Immerse yourself in the emotions made available to you as a result of the birth. The more emotionally available you are, the more whole you will feel. Be grateful for the event, bless the outcome and embrace your new family.

The most valuable advice I can give regarding birth is to *trust the process*. With every fiber of your being be willing to *trust birth* and say YES. It is normal, natural and healthy and yes it is intense. Use your tools and welcome everything birth has to offer.

8

Fathering In Early Infancy

*"It doesn't matter who my father was;
it matters who I remember he was."*

Anne Sexton

Your baby has arrived and you are now, visibly, a father. Welcome dad. Our modern culture rarely provides opportunities to be with infants before the birth of our own child. This new relationship will require time and attention, just like any new relationship. You will want to get to know each other. You will know you are ready for this phase of life because your baby has arrived. You have everything you need to be a great father. You have tremendous value to contribute to your child's life, *that only you can.*

During this early infancy time you will likely be called upon to stretch yourself beyond any previously known boundaries: physical, mental and emotional. This is not something you can practice for in advance. However, the tools and exercises in this book can continue to be of use to you. Breathing and meditation will still have a place. Perhaps meditate while holding your baby or to help calm them when upset occurs. Affirmations and paying attention to your thoughts will also continue to have a role and of course the Fathers' Circle. Notice your stress levels and work to reduce them when necessary. This phase of fathering will introduce additional dimensions to your life which will begin the more active period of your fathering. Be patient with yourself.

Empathy exercise:
A baby during early infancy

Imagine you are a newborn. It is now your initial time outside the womb and you are getting used to a body, people, sounds, sensations and images. You are also needing responses and support from the outside world for the first time: food, warmth and comfort among them. Your nourishment is now from an external source and you may have to exert yourself to get it. You are also building a relationship with your mother, father and perhaps others.

Picture what you would want and need during this phase of your life? Can you imagine what life is like as a newborn baby? How would you feel? How would you want to be handled; by whom and when?

A mother during early infancy

Can you imagine what those initial few months are like as a first-time mother? You may be facing many challenges and insecurities as well as joys. You will be in a deeply intimate experience with this child. You are also no longer 'just' a woman, you are also a mother. Imagine what it is like to have this new little being dependent on you for virtually life itself. What about breastfeeding? What is this like? What about your relationship with the baby's father?

What do you imagine you would want and need to support you during early parenting, as a mother? Explore the possibilities. This will help you to better understand your partner.

Breastfeeding

Breastfeeding can be a profound and deeply intimate part of the relationship between a mother and her infant. It is also a very clever, convenient and easy way to provide the best nourishment possible for a baby. There are mothers who cannot breastfeed or choose not to. As with other aspects of this time it is best if the two of you research and discuss this, and then support the mother in her choice.

There can be no measure of the value of breastfeeding for mother and baby. There are, however, volumes of research which reveal beyond any doubt that it is highly beneficial for both of them, physically and emotionally. Mother's breast milk provides a child with the best possible foundation for his immune system. It also builds on the bonding between mother and child and adds a level of security to the baby's world. A breastfeeding mother is also less likely to experience post-partum depression. This is because of the hormones that come into play as well as the emotional connection it creates between them. The most natural length of time to breastfeed is very individual and best left to each mother and child to determine. Many mothers and babies enjoy breastfeeding for two or more years. Know that your support of the breastfeeding couple is most important and irreplaceable. This is another real form of providing for your family.

Veronika Sophia Robinson, in her book The Drinks are on Me writes, "Breastfeeding is a sacred art. It opens our soul and brings us to a place which connects generations past with future generations."[19]

If your partner is breastfeeding you may have varying responses. You could find it wondrous, sensual and satisfying. You could also feel left out or jealous. You could perceive it as a sexual event that you do not appear to be included in. "Those are my breasts. They have been a source of much sexual pleasure for me and now someone else, possibly even another male, is having his way with them. I am excluded. What about me?" How you respond may surprise you. Be honest with yourself and speak about it with your partner, with care however. Perhaps cuddle with your family when they are breastfeeding. Include yourself, respectfully of course. Be willing to expand your definition of intimacy. Also, go skin to skin with your baby, you will both benefit.

You could write autobiographically about how this is for you. You may discover an underlying cause if you have upset about this. You could also make use of affirmations. The affirmation, "I am included", can be very useful.

Father and Child Bonding

There is a correlation between the amount of time spent parenting and the degree of bonding between parent and child. Because most mothers are spending more time with a newborn than fathers they will seem to have a stronger bond. If you are off to work and doing the physical caretaking of the whole family, your direct time spent with your baby is naturally less. Your connection with your baby, at first, may therefore not seem as strong as the mother's. And the potential may surprise you.

My brother Pete Houser wrote:

After Denise and I came home from the hospital our new son, Jake, would need care at certain times of the day and night. I decided early on that Denise had carried him for nine months and it was now my turn to perform. Denise never got out of bed in the night. As soon as Jake peeped I'd get up to bring him to her for feeding, what could be better, I loved it. Little did I know it at the time but I was catching up on their ultimate bond. That is the only way I can explain the very close relationship I share with my kids. I became a connection point through my participation with them, all the way through high school and even today.

I guess my point is that fathers have a lot of 'work' to do to achieve the bond that mothers get in a different way. Spend as much time as you can, all kinds of time...diaper time, feeding time, sick time, doctor time, play time and sports time. Don't be the father who expects the mother to do all of these things while you bring home the bacon. You can do both and I guarantee you'll be glad you did. Being a father is the single most joyful role I have ever imagined or experienced.

Jonas Himmelstrand wrote:

My wife, Tamara, made some very clear statements on how she wanted to be supported by me, in her role as a mother, around the birth and babyhood of our children. She wanted a homebirth, she wanted family-bed, she wanted the baby to be carried rather than being in a stroller and she wanted long-term breastfeeding and no pacifiers. I realized that the best gift I could give to my children in babyhood was to acknowledge my wife's wishes and support her in every way possible to be the mother she wanted to be. It took me a long time of study and inner work to come to terms with some of her wishes, but I eventually did.

It turned out that Tamara did not have a strong enough back to carry our children, even when they were babies. I stepped in and took the role with pride. As a father you are the 'vice-mother' to your baby. If the mother can't do it or needs to rest, the job is yours and no one can compare to you. I have carried all of our children from birth, through a series of different carriers up, to about three years of age. At that point they have wanted to walk most distances themselves. It has been the greatest pleasure.

During babyhood the baby is often more important to the father than the father to the baby: whose primary needs are met by the mother. Every father needs to feel deep in his heart that this is his child to care for. Having had my children born at home, as I have had the privilege to experience, this bonding is considerably strengthened. During babyhood the father's most vital support to the baby may be in supporting the mother. Being a mother to a baby is a 24/7 job and she needs support from another adult, ideally her baby's father. Having food on the table and a safe home comes first on the list, but also practical and emotional everyday support for the mother is important. In addition the father's connection with the baby will, of course, be enhanced by the father carrying the baby, singing to the baby, talking to the baby and gazing into the beautiful, divine presence of the baby's eyes.

Elmer Postle wrote:

> As a father, my initial understanding of gratitude centered on the idea that children would be grateful to their parents. However, nothing has really prepared me for the gratitude I have to Lucien, my 2 year old son; for what he is giving to me. He is bringing more to my life than I could ever have imagined I would receive from anyone. To receive this gift requires a different perception of how we give to one another. It is not a 'top down' process from parent to child but an exchange between us, for which I am deeply grateful.

I highly recommend mothers and fathers 'wear' their baby. There are any number of slings, pouches and carriers which are great for this. It provides a closeness to and security for your new baby that is unachievable otherwise. I am also in favor of co-sleeping, a very wonderful experience for the whole family. For more information on 'attachment' parenting see Resources section and the internet.

Allow yourself to receive all of the love your baby has for you and know that your love is received by him as well. Remember, "My baby loves me". Your participation is important for you and your baby, it is different than the mother's, and it will change over time. Know that by you supporting their connection your presence is felt and appreciated and your bond will deepen.

Inner Strength

Sometimes you may be called upon to develop gifts you didn't know you had. After my first son's intense birth, Kathryn was very poorly. She was physically and emotionally bankrupt. Anandas was unsettled at best or crying and once asleep would only stay sleeping if he was being held. Breastfeeding was painful for Kathryn and not going well also. She was detached and withdrawn because of the emotional and physical impact of the birth.

The house we were building was not finished so we were living in a summer cottage, in December. Within a few days after the birth the temperature dropped below freezing and it snowed. Our heat source was a wood burning stove which was ineffective for the conditions. Also the water pipes froze so we had no running water. I spent my days acquiring firewood and hauling water from the pump house. In between these activities I fixed meals, changed (and hand-washed) diapers and tried to comfort my family.

My world was concentrated on my family and doing whatever it took. I notice that we will typically find the inner resources to handle what we are asked to, if we are committed. You will also.

Although intense, this was a very intimate and

bonding experience for us. The birthing time carries with it a commonality of experience which can solidify a family, regardless of the appearance. Within a couple of weeks we found a holistic practitioner, a chiropractor/ iridologist. Iridology is the study of the eyes' 'map' of our body's physical health. He looked into Anandas' eyes and saw a hip and shoulder dislocation and with two gentle movements Anandas was at peace. He looked into Kathryn's eyes and saw that there was a bit of placenta still in her womb and gave her a mineral douche to use. Within a short time she expelled this and her body healed. The emotional effects took longer but they healed as well, through willingness and therapeutic support.

Expanding Your Relationship

You and your partner are expanding your relationship *and* including another person. The leap from two people in a relationship to three (or more if there are other children) is significant and may have more impact than you initially realize. It can be a most endearing and profound shift. One aspect of this, from a modern fathering perspective, is that you can cradle your infant, through cradling your partner. I suggest you do this literally as well as metaphorically. The loving care you give to her also includes by its' very nature, caring for your child. This is a really important point because integrating it will allow you to feel more included. For a mother and child to have your support in this way is very important and valuable.

Notice if this expansion comes easily for you or if you find yourself struggling or reacting in some way. You may expose previously un-revealed 'negative' thoughts or uncomfortable feelings. Many of us were not held, physically or emotionally, as much or in the way that we would have liked. It is common that needy feelings come up at this time. There can be a tendency to try to get these needs met through your partner. With her attention elsewhere you could feel like you are being left out. This can appear as jealousy of the baby. You could also find yourself trying to stop various levels of intimacy within your family as a reaction. If you have this experience, be kind to yourself and speak with your partner about it.

You may want to create an affirmation and work with it to achieve more peace around this issue. "I am enough, I do enough, I have enough", could work for you. "I am included", "I am important". Seek support for yourself and write about it.

Fatherhood has the potential to be a highly intimate experience. To hold your tiny baby in your arms; to experience their fragile nature and look into their eyes and know that they love you, trust you and depend on you for their very existence is remarkably intimate. At times, when my Fathers-To-Be colleague Elmer is with his son Lucien, he imagines his own father holding him, as he is holding his young son, and finds this profoundly satisfying and supportive. This makes for a lovely picture in my mind. How wonderful can you imagine your fathering?

The quality of your presence in your family is invaluable. Your willingness to do whatever it takes is deeply felt by them. Fathering a family is something you will grow into and get more comfortable with through time and experience. It is a journey and not a destination. Consider parenting to be a process of refinement.

Following is an excerpt from a lovely book which supports parents during a baby's upset.

CALMS-Five Simple Steps to Harmony
From the book <u>What Babies Want</u> by
Carrie Contey Ph.D. and Debby Takikawa D.C.

You want to do what is best for your baby, and like most parents, you're not always quite sure what that is. CALMS is a set of tools to provide you with ideas about how to stay connected to yourself and your child as you learn to understand what it is your child is trying to communicate to you when they are distressed. A child in upset is one of parenting's most challenging occurrences and CALMS can help you through these events. "CALMS" is a way of being rather than a mode of doing. Here is a brief overview of the CALMS method.[20]

CALMS

C *Check in with yourself*
>   The first step in calming your crying baby is to check in with yourself, take a pause and identify your own feelings.

A *Allow a breath*
>   Take several deep breaths and allow things to simply be just as they are in this moment.

L *Listen to your baby*
>   Take a moment or two just to wonder what you think your baby is trying to say.

M *Make contact, mirror feelings*
>   Let your baby know you hear him and you see that he is sad or angry, frustrated or frantic.

S *Soothe your baby*
>   Now is the time to do the rocking, walking, swaddling, breastfeeding and soothing that wasn't working earlier.

Bonus Fathers

There are also men who have answered the call of being a dad even though they are not birth fathers. This includes step-fathers, grandfathers, uncles, older brothers, teachers, coaches, scout leaders, spiritual fathers

(Priests, Rabbis, Vicars, Ministers, Monks, etc.), and other men (and women) who assume responsibility for the guidance and support of young people. My brother, Mike, has no children of his own yet he fulfils fathering through his charity work with organizations that support children in need. The contribution of all such fathers is highly valuable to our society. I acknowledge them for their love and support of our children, and society's future.

Father's Compass
Looking Ahead

How do you want to be remembered as a father? Contemplate for a moment this scenario. It is decades from now and your child is asked the question, "What was your father like when you were growing up?" Can you imagine what they will say? You actually have a choice. What if you have the opportunity to write the answer to that question yourself and influence your own legacy as a father?

How do you want to be remembered as a father? If you like, you could write your own fathering declaration. What is your vision for your fathering? This will be different for everyone. It could be a few words or phrases, a list, or even several paragraphs. You may also want to update this as the years go by.

This declaration could become your personal Father's Compass. Consider coming back to this declaration regularly as you grow and practice being a father. It could help you navigate the terrain of fathering and keep you on course, especially during the challenging times. If you already have children, it is never too late. A new direction can be chosen at any time. Gifts of this nature are always welcome.

When I was growing up I always had a compass. I found it fascinating that something that simple could be so useful and potentially valuable. You could also gift your child with an actual compass, as a symbol of your commitment and something special between you. One comes in the Fathers-To-Be Tool Kit.

When your children come of age, or they are about to become a parent themselves, you could present them with your personal Father's Compass. Imagine having a conversation with your child about parenting, with your intention as a father as the central theme. Naturally, this works equally well for sons and daughters. Our daughters are learning about mothering from their mothers. They are also learning about fathering, and what to expect from a future partner they may have children with, from their father. Sons are, of course, learning from their mothers what it means to be a mother, for future reference. Mothers-to-be can also benefit greatly by much of the information in this book.

Consider that your children will be bestowing the very same gifts they received from you on to your grandchildren, great grandchildren and so on for generations. Your practice of a Father's Compass could become a treasured family heirloom that is passed on for generations. How do you want to be remembered as a father? What if you have a choice and what if you get to make it every day of your life as a father?

Conscious Evolution

We could also view parenting from an evolutionary perspective. An aspect of human evolution could be dependent on us, individually and collectively, through our practice as parents. The application of this practice is then archived and passed on to the next generation, hopefully with more grace each time around. I was told recently by an expectant woman that her husband has always said to her about his future fathering, "I am going to do it differently". I have heard this from many men. Well, that resolve plus awareness, guidance and high-quality support is all that is required for our evolutionary advancement as parents. The customary view is that we are at the effect of evolution. What if, instead, we are actually instruments of it?

With first hand knowledge of four generations of Houser fathers I can testify as to the actuality of evolution in fathering. As I witness my own sons' fathering I am deeply moved by their level of commitment and participation with their children. Let's embrace future generations, today.

A Great Beginning

I invite you to continue exploring what you really want for yourself and your family. As a father, you have an unprecedented opportunity to influence the health and wellbeing of your family as well as human culture.

You now have new knowledge and new choices. Equipped with a fresh understanding you can help to *provide* for your partner and child and *protect* them in ways that will be as supportive as possible. The blending of love and knowledge equals wisdom. The application of this wisdom is the essence of fathering.

Resist the temptation to judge your performance. This is generally a perception of good or bad. Evaluation instead will allow you to learn from each phase and build on your fathering knowledge and skills. Avoid any tendency to think you must become super-dad. Be willing to forgive yourself when things do not go to plan or you experience upset. You are actually a father-becoming. This means, among other things, you are a work in progress. Your family is growing up together. Be gentle and kind with yourself. Ask for support when you need it. By simply exposing yourself to new concepts, reading this book and engaging in the exercises, you have already become a better father. Notice your thoughts and what your emotions, your body's sensations and feedback from life are telling you. Work with that information to make adjustments in order to produce the results you want. This is a journey to explore and enjoy, with love and your commitment to your family as your guide.

What you achieve on the journey of fatherhood can only be measured in your family's hearts, and in truth it is immeasurable. The first step is awareness and you have already crossed that bridge. Congratulations.

Take the risk to love with every ounce of your being, to share your gifts and receive the ones your children have to offer you. Welcome to Fatherhood!

A new father has arrived.

Afterward

Creativity and Pregnancy
By Binnie A. Dansby

Binnie is my wife and a fellow pioneer in conscious birthing and living practices.

The process of conception, pregnancy and birth is a most available metaphor for creativity. When we have an idea, we have conceived. If we add energy and time and attention to the idea, we are pregnant with the possibility. Continued persistence will bring forth a result, a **birth**. *In the light of this understanding I always encourage pregnant fathers to be aware of the creative energy that is available when their partner is pregnant. At no other time are we more creative than in the process of 'becoming'. I consider the human body to be the most sophisticated and beautiful of artworks. The energy that was necessary to paint the Sistine Chapel does not come close to the energy that is necessary to create a human body. Each father-to-be is in direct contact with that energy when sleeping, when making love and when simply being in daily life. Awareness is the key to the access and use of this valuable resource.*

Many years ago I taught a class called the Conscious Birthing Program in Santa Monica, California. Fathers were always welcome and typically comprised one third of those present. The intention of the class was to facilitate the release of any fears regarding birth. We explored each partner's birth experience as the source of his or her thoughts about birth. Sometimes these thoughts are held just below the level of conscious awareness. I used gentle breathwork, visualization, and affirmation to help people to remember, release and heal. We also gave attention to society's thinking about birth and what the people in their lives were telling them about birth. This supported them to acknowledge the influence of the environment on their thoughts and behavior.

During this time I had a private client in my counseling and breathwork practice who was a screenwriter with 'writer's block'. In one of our sessions I suddenly suggested that he come to the Wednesday morning Conscious Birthing class. He was, understandably, in doubt about my sanity, and I admit, I had my doubts, as well. Given some thought, I knew the reason for my invitation was to expose him to all the creative energy generated by 10 to 15 pregnant women. With encouragement he came and continued to join us every Wednesday for several months. In a very short time one fourth of the participants in the program were creative artists of some form. Everyone was pregnant, some with ideas and some with human beings and new lives.

It has been a privilege to work with couples who chose to use the energy of pregnancy to start up new businesses, build new homes, and take art classes together. One couple decided to do The Artist's Way, by Julia Cameron, as they were creating a baby together. Another went to French class as a couple. Other couples took Tango and Salsa lessons. They all expressed how easy and enjoyable creative pursuits were for them during pregnancy.

An added advantage to learning and creating during pregnancy is that the baby will have an affinity for the language or the activity when they are of an appropriate age. A German woman whom I met spoke English with a British accent. I asked if she had lived in England. She told me that she had not. With further inquiry it was revealed that her parents lived in London during her mother's pregnancy with her. They were learning English and speaking it for most of the 9 months. They returned to Germany only a week or so before the birth. She reported that one of her easiest classes in school was her English class.

An essential aspect of creativity is curiosity. What do you really want for yourself and your partner and your children? What gives you pleasure? What is something you have been longing to learn about? What is something you have wanted to do with your partner, just the two of you? You have a new life adventure ahead. Be curious about what is happening with your partner. Be curious about the possibilities of giving birth, the world over. Be curious about how to best nourish your pregnant partner and your baby. Be curious about 'fathering' and parenting practices in other cultures. Have fun during pregnancy. Explore the creative possibilities in all parts of your life. Expand and grow during this intense and precious time and the future will reflect your efforts and commitment.

Protecting the Cave
By Patrick M. Houser

The ancient archetype of a father at birth is that he stands guard at the opening to the cave to protect the birthing mother and their child. As we move through time he comes closer to the actual location of the birth itself; waiting, protecting. Then, in the late 20th century he enters the room and becomes involved. His first role was to protect the family from danger; wild animals or perhaps other tribes people...survival. As birth became more industrialized his role has altered. Could it be that the father is entering the birthing room for a more primal reason than we would like to think?

Is there a chance the danger is now coming from even closer to the mother and baby? Could it now be coming from inside the room itself? Has interference from our modern approach to birth, a natural physiological process, reached the point where fathers are now needed to intercede, to protect in a new way? Caesarean rates in some countries have escalated to as high as eighty percent. Interventions of every un-imaginable kind are rampant and much of what is being 'done to' the mother and child is unnecessary and pre-emptive.

What if a reason has evolved to have the father in the birthing room, in addition to bonding and support? Suppose that a modern form of a father's protection is to guard against the excessive interference of people, equipment and artificial drugs into the very ordinary process of birth. Many interventions at birth are the result of over educated professionals, with good intentions, who are medically trained to intervene in a non-medical process.

'*Humanity cannot invent a drug that can work better than a mothers' body can manufacture or a knife that is sharper than her instinctual nature.*'

If a mother is properly protected and an environment is provided that is safe and warm and free from unnecessary interventions, distractions and interruptions; questions, examinations and conversations, she can get on with the business of being in her 'instinctual brain' and access all of the hormones and inner resources she and her body need to birth her baby in love, safety and empowerment.

When it comes to hospital births a fathers biggest challenge/dilemma is how to navigate/negotiate the gauntlet of this totally foreign environment. You will face emotional and physical situations as never before. These will pertain to you directly as well as the ones you love, want to protect and want the best for. There is no 'good or right' answer as to how to do this. Prepare yourself as best you can, get reasonable and satisfactory answers to your questions and remember to stay centered (use your tools) and above all trust your partners ability to give birth.

The Spirit of Fatherhood
By Patrick M. Houser

Spirituality is another element of becoming a father. The child you are caring for is more than just a body. There is also an invisible yet vital element that is their soul or spirit. This lies at the very core of your child's being. It contains his or her creative potential and highest ideals.

Like all aspects of a child it needs to be nurtured. Be aware of the soul within and hold it as you hold your child's body: gently, kindly and with the greatest respect. Embrace their spirit and know they embrace yours. When you hold your new born baby in your arms you can feel the deepest spiritual connection you share. The miracle of pregnancy, birth and early infancy has the possibility to soften and transform the strongest and most formidable of men.

Embrace your spiritual potential as a father. You can provide the framework in which your child's spirit can unfold. Providing the security of a safe home and a structure for them to expand into are key. Going to work each day and looking after your children may seem mundane but it is spirituality in action and central to their wellbeing. Virtues such as compassion, unconditional love and forgiveness are spiritual lessons you can also provide. This unique blend of mind, body and spirit which is your child needs direction that only you, their father, can provide.

Whatever guidance you seek to give your child, be the teaching. Children learn about respect by being respected. They learn about trust by being trusted. Children learn best through example.

Rather than trying to mould them into your likeness, what if you listened very carefully and let them tell you who they want to become? In this way you are not so much teaching them but supporting the awakening of their soul. This happens by finding more and more ways to say YES to who they are, how they are and who they want to become. Do you best to restrict the use of the word no. It is non-constructive and can be soul destroying, safety aside. If we recognize the spiritual nature of each of us then we only need to love our children beyond all measure, trust the process and watch them unfold.

The Dalai Lama is the spiritual head of Tibetan Buddhism. From a very young age he was raised as 'someone special'. He was told that he had an extraordinary purpose in this life and that he would accomplish great things. He was treated with tremendous respect by everyone. It was also clear that this was his destiny and he should study and learn as much as possible, so as to do his best in his life's work. Look at who he has become. He teaches peace through everything he says and does, even with his people's oppressors. In my opinion this is no coincidence. Putting aside religious beliefs or practices imagine the outcome, individually and collectively, if every child is raised similarly. What if all children are told that they are someone special, they have unique gifts and an extraordinary life purpose to fulfill; one that only they can? What if all children are treated with that level of care and respect, by everyone? Imagine.

Also consider the possibility that your children are destined to be your greatest teachers. A wise old soul may be found in the youngest of bodies. This concept may be just the opposite of what you might have thought. What if you became the student and allowed yourself to learn from him or her? Listen carefully.

Be open to the *Spirit of Fatherhood* and all it has to offer. The rewards will be great. It is *all* a spiritual experience. *Thank you God!*

Acknowledgements

I acknowledge those who have preceded me; my ancestors in the fields of fathering, pregnancy, birth and birth psychology. Their guidance and contribution is invaluable.

I will forever have heartfelt gratitude to my father and mother, Jim and Nancy. Their great passion was their children and their family, thank you. I am also grateful to my grandparents for sharing their love so freely. And for my siblings, Pete, Ann, Mike, Tom and Jim; what a pleasure it is to call you sister and brothers.

I am particularly grateful for Kathryn Houser, my former wife, the mother of my children and fellow life and parent voyager. Thank you for the love, adventure and the children we share.

My deepest appreciation goes to Anandas and Jeremy, my beloved sons and teachers. Gratitude as well to my grandsons: Christian, Jackson and Carmine for their loving presence. Thank you also to my 'bonus sons', Dan and Rob Kirkpatrick.

I greatly appreciate the proof reading and editorial support I have received from Richard Branson, Mary Britton, Douglas Crawford, Maya Morgan, Laura Shanley, Geoffrey

Montague-Smith, Roma Norriss, Laura & Hal Uplinger and Sean Williams.

Much love and deep appreciation to my dear friend and brilliant supporter Helene Smith-Harris.

Simenon Honoré has been my editor and self-proclaimed 'midwife' on this project. I am deeply grateful for his wisdom, editorial precision, professionalism and the scope of his insight. In addition, for his recognition and clear vision of my soul's purpose as well as his own.

My deep personal and professional gratitude to Elmer Postle, my friend, colleague and Fathers-To-Be co-founder, for the emotion and intelligence that he brings to everything he does. I am especially grateful for his contribution to this book through editing and content. His consistent support towards excellence in this offering and other of our Fathers-To-Be projects is invaluable.

My extra special gratitude and acknowledgement goes to my wife, Binnie A. Dansby. Binnie is a gifted teacher (in the fields of pregnancy, birth, birth psychology and personal development), mentor and loving presence in my life. She has had more influence on me and this book than can be articulated but/ and THANK YOU Binnie!

References

1. What Good Are Dads, Lewis www.fathersdirect.com
2. Equal Opportunities Commission, www.eoc.org.uk
3. Fathers Direct, www.fatherhoodinstitute.co.uk
4. The Secret Life of the Unborn Child, Verny & Kelly
5. A Course in Miracles, Foundation for Inner Peace
6. Birth and Beyond, Dr. Yehudi Gordon
7. Breathwork, www.sourcebreath.com,
        www.breathwork.com, www.holotropic.com,
        www.transformationsusa.com
8. Heal Your Body, Louise Hay
9. Maternal Emotions and Human Development,
        Lipton Ph.D www.birthpsychology.com
10. Unassisted Childbirth, Laura Shanley
11. The Mind of Your Newborn Baby, Chamberlain
12. Birth a History, Tina Cassidy
13. The Truth About Birth, Laura Shanley
14. Magical Child, Joseph Chilton Pearce
15. Ecstatic Birth...conceive the possibility, Dansby
        Educational DVD
16. Psycho-Technology of Pregnancy and Labor, Pre
        and Perinatal Psychology and Medicine,
        1988, Dr. Thomas Verny
17. Journal of AMA, 2007 study, McMaster University
18. The Healing of Birth, Invitation to Intimacy, Postle
19. The Drinks are on Me, Veronika Sophia Robinson
20. What Babies Want, Contey & Takikawa

Resources

APPPAH, www.birthpsychology.com
Attachment Parenting Int, www.attachmentparenting.org
Birthing From Within www.birthingfromwithin.com
Birthing the Future, www.birthingthefuture.com
Bradley Method, The, www.bradleybirth.com
Castellino Prenatal/Birth Tr,www.castellinotraining.com
DONA, Doulas of North America, www.dona.org
Ecstatic Pregnancy & Birth, www.ecstaticbirth.com
Fathers websites: www: FathersToBe.org, fatherville.com,
fathers.com, fathersworld.com, dictionaryfordads.org,
thedadman.com, azffc.org, bcnd.org, menstuff.org,

mrdad.com, dadsadventure.com, fatherlove.com
HypnoBirthing, www.hypnobirthing.com
KPM Approach to Children, www.kpmapproach.org
La Leche League, www.laleche.org
Lamaze Birth Preparation, www.lamaze.org
Touch the Future, www.ttfuture.org
The Mother Magazine, www.themothermagazine.co.uk
Waterbirth International, www.waterbirth.org
Zero to Three, www.zerotothree.org

More Sources

Becoming a Father, Singh & Newburn, NCT
Being Dad, DVD www.beingdadusa.com
Best Things Fathers Do, Will Glennon
Birth as an American Rite of Passage, Davis-Floyd
Birth As We Know It, DVD, www.birthintobeing.com
Birth Without Fear, Dr. Grantly Dick-Read
Birth Without Violence, Fredric Leboyer
Birthing Fathers, Richard K. Reed
Continuum Concept, Jean Liedloff
Education Begins Before Birth, Aivanhov
Embracing Your Father, Dr. Linda Nielsen
Father and Child Reunion, Warren Farrell Ph.D.
Gentle Birth, Gentle Mothering, Sarah Buckley M.D.
Gifts of Our Fathers, Thomas R. Verny M.D.
Heart To Heart Parenting, Robin Grille
HypnoBirthing, The Mongan Method, Marie Mongan
Immaculate Deception, Suzanne Arms
Including New Fathers, www.fatherhoodinstitute.co.uk
Molecules of Emotion, Candace Pert Ph.D.
Nurturing the Unborn Child, Verny & Weintraub
Orgasmic Birth, DVD, Debra Pascali-Bonaro
Parenting for a Peaceful World, Robin Grille
The Biology of Belief, Bruce Lipton Ph.D.
The Biology of Transcendence, J. C. Pearce
The Expectant Father, Brott & Ash
The Father's Home Birth Handbook, Leah Hazard
The Modern Mom's Guide to Dads, Hilling & Rutherford
What Babies Want, DVD, Takikawa
Why Love Matters, Sue Gerhardt

Social Action

Sample Letter

Do you think it is reasonable that our hospitals, schools and communities should offer classes for expectant dads? Below is a sample letter that you could use as a model to stimulate governments, organizations and institutions to offer them. *We* need to take action if *we* want change to occur.

Dear _____

I am an expectant dad in our local community. I have searched for fatherhood classes to help me prepare for my new role and have found little or nothing available. I would like to have the opportunity to attend classes to help me to be the best father I can be.

I imagine having discussion forums with other fathers to further my understanding and perhaps mentors to help me get my questions answered and concerns handled.

Would you please arrange for workshops, classes, mentoring and general support for me and other expectant dads in our community? Please feel free to contact me.

Sincerely,

(name)
(address, phone, email)

Modeled on a letter from, <u>The Modern Mom's Guide to Dads.</u>

Furthermore

F2B workshops for parents are available in the UK and elsewhere, on request.

Patrick Houser is available for counseling, coaching (phone/SKYPE), speaking engagements, workshops (DONA CEU's available) for birth professionals/educators and consulting on fatherhood and whole family policies and procedures anywhere.

There is tremendous value to be gained from each of our experiences. Other fathers and mothers can learn from them. We are collecting *your stories*, the source can be kept anonymous if you prefer. Photos are also welcome. Please email us. Share your challenges and your joys. info@fatherstobe.org

Also Available

<u>Fathers-To-Be Tool Kit</u>, Essential & fun items and information for new and expectant dad's
<u>Fathers-To-Be Handbook</u>, multiple copies at whole sale prices for childbirth educators, midwives, doulas, websites & stores
<u>Having a Baby is the Most Natural Thing in the World</u> CD by Binnie A. Dansby
<u>Rhythm of Life,</u> CD by Binnie A. Dansby
<u>Ecstatic Birth...conceive the possibility</u> educational DVD by Binnie A. Dansby
<u>The Healing of Birth: Invitation to Intimacy</u>, documentary DVD by Elmer Postle
And much, much more at:
www.creativelifesystems.com
www.FathersToBe.org

Father2Father

Fathers-To-Be is building
a mentoring/support network;
fathers coming together in living rooms
around the world for mutual support.
See website for details to find a get
together near you *or to hosting one*.

www.FathersToBe.org

One Baby
Two Parents
Supporting Early Parenthood

We are promoting an awareness
campaign to emphasize the importance
of our children and the valuable
contribution each parent
has to offer them.

www.onebabytwoparents.org

The SOURCE Foundation International
is a UK based registered charity
conceived to:
*Promote health and provide healing from
preconception to birth and throughout life.*
Funding for our work
is needed and welcome.
www.FathersToBe.org